\TE DUE

Henry Louis Gates, Jr.

AFRICAN-AMERICAN LEADERS

Henry Louis Gates, Jr.

Marylou Morano Kjelle

CHELSEA HOUSE PUBLISHERS

A Haights Cross Communications Company

Philadelphia

CHELSEA HOUSE PUBLISHERS
VP, New Product Development Sally Cheney
Director of Production Kim Shinners
Creative Manager Takeshi Takahashi
Manufacturing Manager Diann Grasse

Staff for HENRY LOUIS GATES, JR.
Editor Sally Cheney
Editorial Assistant Josh Spiegel
Production Editor Megan Emery
Assistant Photo Editor Noelle Nardone
Series & Cover Designer Terry Mallon
Layout EJB Publishing

A Haights Cross Communications Company
www.chelseahouse.com

First Printing

1 3 5 7 9 8 6 4 2

Library of Congress Cataloging-in-Publication Data

Kjelle, Marylou Morano.
  Henry Louis Gates, Jr. / by Marylou Morano Kjelle.
    p. cm. — (African American leaders)
Summary: A biography of the noted literary historian, critic, author,
and scholar who taught at many leading universities before becoming
head of the African American Studies department at Harvard. Includes
bibliographical references and index.
  ISBN 0-7910-7687-3
  1. Gates, Henry Louis—Juvenile literature. 2. African American
scholars—Biography—Juvenile literature. 3. Critics—United States—
Biography—Juvenile literature. [1. Gates, Henry Louis. 2. Critics. 3.
Educators. 4. Authors, American. 5. African Americans—Biography.] I.
Title. II. Series.
  PS29.G28K58 2003
  810.9'896073—dc22
                                              2003014152

Table of Contents

INTRODUCTION

Beginning with the publication of the series *Black Americans of Achievement* nearly twenty years ago, Chelsea House Publishers made a commitment to publishing biographies for young adults that celebrated the lives of many of the country's most outstanding African Americans. The mix of individuals whose lives we covered was eclectic, to say the least. Some were well known—Dr. Martin Luther King, Jr., for example—although others we covered might be lesser known—Madam C.J. Walker, for example. Some—like the actor Danny Glover—were celebrities with legions of adoring fans. It mattered not what an individual's "star" quality might be, or how well known they were to the general public. What mattered was the life of the individual— their actions, their deeds, and, ultimately, their influence on the lives of others and our nation, as a whole. By telling the life stories of these unique Americans, we hoped to tell the story of how ordinary individuals are transformed by extraordinary circumstances to people of greatness. We hoped that the special lives we covered would inspire and encourage our young-adult readers to go out in the world and make a positive difference; and judging from the many wonderful letters that we have received over the years from students, librarians, and teachers about our *Black Americans of Achievement* biographies, we are certain that many of our readers did just that!

Now, some twenty years later, we are proud to release this new series of biographies, *African-American Leaders,* which we hope will make a similar mark on the lives of our young-adult readers. The individuals whose lives we cover in this first set of six books are all contemporary

African-American leaders. As these individuals are all living, the biographers made every attempt to interview their subjects so they could provide first-hand accounts and interesting anecdotes about each subject's life.

After reading about the likes of Henry Louis Gates, Jr., Cornel West, Condoleezza Rice, Carol Moseley-Braun, Eleanor Holmes Norton, and Benjamin Hooks, we think you will agree that the lives of these African-American leaders are remarkable. By overcoming the barriers that racism placed in their paths, they are an example of the power and resiliency of the human spirit and an inspiration to us all.

The Editor
Chelsea House Publishers

1

Freeing
a Voice

> "If *The Bondwoman's Narrative* was based upon actu-
> al experience, it could be our first pristine encounter
> with the unadulterated 'voice' of a fugitive slave,
> exactly as she wrote and edited it."
>
> —Henry Louis Gates, Jr., "The Fugitive,"
> The *New Yorker*, February 18 & 25, 2002

"It may be that I assume to[o] much responsibility in attempting to write these pages. The world will probably say so, and I am aware of my deficiencies. I am neither clever, nor learned, nor talented...."

So begins the book, *The Bondwoman's Narrative* by Hannah Crafts. Believed to be written before the Civil War, it is probably the earliest known novel written by an African-American female slave, and quite possibly the earliest novel written by an African-American female anywhere. Within its pages is the story of a North Carolinian planta-

8

tion house slave, and her escape via the underground railroad to a community of free blacks in New Jersey.

The Bondwoman's Narrative was discovered by Henry Louis Gates, Jr., the chair of Afro-American Studies at Harvard University and director of the University's W.E.B. Du Bois Institute for Afro-American Research. A collector of African-American manuscripts and memorabilia, he often browses the New York-based Swann Galleries catalog of "Printed & Manuscript African-Americana" for soon-to-be auctioned artifacts of black culture. In February 2001, he came across an unusual offering. It read:

"Unpublished Original Manuscript . . . a fictionalized biography, written in an effusive style, purporting to be the story of the early life and escape of one Hannah Crafts, a mulatto, born in Virginia . . ."

THE DISCOVERY OF A LIFETIME

The full title of the manuscript was listed as *The Bondwoman's Narrative by Hannah Crafts, a Fugitive Slave, recently Escaped from North Carolina.* "It is uncertain that this work is written by a 'negro,'" the description continued, but it consisted of 21 chapters and was written by "someone intimately familiar with the areas in the South where the narrative takes place. Her escape route is one sometimes used by run-aways." The manuscript contained 301 handwritten pages and was clothbound. It had come from the private collection of Dorothy Porter Wesley, a scholar of antebellum black literature. Wesley was a historian and librarian at Howard University in Washington, D.C. who had died in 1995. She had acquired the manuscript in 1948 from Emily Driscoll, a rare book and autograph dealer. Driscoll had acquired it from a traveling book dealer, who told her the manuscript had originated in New Jersey.

Gates's interest in collecting early African-American manuscripts and memorabilia took an interesting turn when he discovered that one of the manuscripts he had acquired, *The Bondwoman's Narrative by Hannah Crafts,* was the earliest handwritten account of a female runaway slave. Here we see a smiling Gates after he delivered a speech at the University of North Carolina-Chapel Hill, where he talked about finding the 150-year-old manuscript.

Gates was the only bidder on the manuscript, and he acquired it for $8,500. Upon receipt of the document, he found it to be sheets of paper folded in half with the front and back of each half making up a page. The pages were yellowed and the brown-inked handwriting faded. An attempt at self-editing had been made, as each page

10

held various corrections, crossed out words, and pasted-in inserts. The writing ran into the binding, indicating that the book had been bound after it had been written. From references to classical literature throughout the manuscript, it was obvious that the writer was well-read, not unusual for educated slaves who worked in homes that contained a library. Indeed, in *The Bondwoman's Narrative*, Crafts explains her literacy as the result of self-teaching, looking at old books and newspapers, and eventually becoming the student of a white woman, the poor wife of a laborer who lived in a nearby cottage.

While many other examples of nineteenth century African-American literature have been uncovered over the years, Gates's discovery of *The Bondwoman's Narrative* was historically significant. Not only was it the earliest discovered account by a female runaway slave, it was the only known holographic (handwritten) account of a runaway known to exist. Even the well-known writings of runaway slaves such as Frederick Douglass and Sojurner Truth did not survive as holographs, only as printed accounts.

An ex-slave's unedited, handwritten manuscript would offer literary historians and scholars a previously unavailable opportunity to study the literacy level of at least one slave. The manuscript could be researched prior to the professional editing that other African-American works had undergone preceding publishing. Gates wrote in The *New Yorker* magazine in 2002: "If *The Bondwoman's Narrative* was based upon actual experience, it could be our first pristine encounter with the unadulterated 'voice' of a fugitive slave, exactly as she wrote and edited it."

THE FAMOUS MR. GATES

It is unsurprising that Gates discovered *The Bondwoman's Narrative*. A literary historian, critic, and leading scholar of African-American Studies for three decades, Gates is widely considered the originator and definer of black literary criticism. He has edited anthologies and written encyclopedias, and he is the author of more than a dozen books. He has written scores of essays and articles on African and African-American issues including slavery, race, feminism, and cultural identity. He has produced documentaries for public television on his travels through the African continent. Over the years, he and his colleagues working on the Black Periodical Literature Project have authenticated and restored the work of thousands of black authors. These efforts have raised the author's writings to the standards of contemporary American and African-American literature.

Gates has been called "the most visible and influential present-day American humanist." His own writings, as well as his discovery and authentication of the historically significant writings of others, have catapulted him into a limelight seldom experienced by academics.

One of Gates's most significant discoveries came about in 1982, when he found and authenticated *Our Nig; Or, Sketches from the Life of a Free Black, in a Two-Story White House, North: Showing That Slavery's Shadows Fall Even There*, a novel written by an indentured black servant, Harriet E. Wilson, in 1859. Until the discovery of *The Bondwoman's Narrative*, Wilson's book was considered to be the first known novel in the United States written by an African-American female.

LITERARY DETECTIVE WORK

Gates began making exhaustive inquiries into the

To determine the authenticity of *The Bondwoman's Narrative* manuscript, Gates set about researching the people, events, and places that Crafts described. An important person in Crafts's life was John Hill Wheeler (pictured here), a notorious pre-Civil War slave holder and assistant secretary to President Franklin Pierce.

authenticity of *The Bondwoman's Narrative* and its author. He consulted with professional historical document specialists to determine the age of the document. Studying the manuscript's paper, ink, binding, and style of writing, it was determined to have been written in the 1850s. The absence of references to the Civil War supports this theory.

Using the United States census records, the Mormon Family Library in Salt Lake City, and the Library of Congress, Gates explored several avenues to authenticate the author and the people and places about which she wrote. Crafts accurately recorded mid-nineteenth century life in Virginia, where she was born, and on the North Carolina plantation, where she lived as the property of John Hill Wheeler, a notorious pre-Civil War slaveholder. In the mid-1850s Wheeler served as assistant secretary to President Franklin Pierce and as the United States ambassador to Nicaragua. Crafts also writes of Washington, D.C., where she often traveled with her master and mistress on government business. Many of the scenes depicted in *The Bondwoman's Narrative* coincided with events found in Wheeler's diary and other papers researched by Gates.

While Gates was able to ascertain from historical censuses that many of the characters named in the novel were actual people, he was unable to find a specific person that he could credit as being Hannah Crafts. Gates believes the author's "vagueness actually lends authenticity, and her reluctance to reveal the specifics of Hannah's escape route validates her fear of being caught and returned to her owner."

Despite the mystery of the author's identity, in 2002, a century and a half after it was written, Gates edited and published *The Bondwoman's Narrative*, allowing a voice long silenced to be heard. In doing so, he validated the significance of the African-American past and a cultural heritage, which through his southern roots, he can call his own.

2

"Skippy"

"She [Gates' mother] and Daddy would provide the best
for us, so that no white person could put us down or
keep us out for reasons of appearance, color aside. The
rest was up to us, once we got in those white places."
—Henry Louis Gates, Jr.,
Colored People: A Memoir

Nestled in the Allegheny Mountains, and surrounded by
the Potomac River Valley lies Piedmont, West Virginia,
the birthplace of Louis Smith Gates, the birth name given to
Henry Louis Gates, Jr. The word *piedmont* means "at the foot
of the mountain," and it is a fitting name for the picturesque
little town, which is situated on the side of a hill where the
mountains meet the river. Piedmont sits on the banks of the
Potomac, the same river that runs through Washington,
D.C., and the two locations are separated by approximately
120 miles, with Piedmont located to the northwest.

Born in Piedmont, West Virginia, young Henry (seen here in this 1950 photo) grew up in a warm, nurturing family environment. In addition to his immediate family, Gates was fortunate to have his extended family living within five miles of his home.

Today, a little over 1,000 people live in the scenic village of hills and valleys, and about one-third of the population is African American. When Henry was born on September 16, 1950, Piedmont was a flourishing town whose population of approximately 2,550 people, was an ethnic mixture of Irish, Italians, and "colored people," a term frequently used at the time to designate African Americans. Many of the townspeople's ancestors had arrived in Piedmont in the early 1900s, drawn by the promise of employment in the Westvaco Paper Mill, the town's main employer, which opened in 1888.

A SEGREGATED WORLD

Although Piedmont's ethnically diverse residents lived together in peace, each group knew its boundaries, both geographically and socially. The Italians and Irish lived on "Irish Hill." The wealthiest people lived in the spacious Victorian, Queen Anne, and Federal-style homes that perched on upper East Hampton Street. Other ethnic neighborhoods were scattered throughout the town. Piedmont's African Americans lived in established and tight-knit communities in three distinct neighborhoods: downtown on Back Street, up on the hill on Erin Street, or on Pearl Street, also known as Rat Tail Road, so named because the twists and turns the road took as it winded its way from the top of the hill to the bottom of the valley resembled a rat's tail.

The 1950s and 1960s were years in which the United States made great strides in civil rights. Yet, change came slowly to the small, conservative town of Piedmont where people were set in their ways. Henry lived his first few years in a segregated society, where the law prevented blacks from eating in restaurants like the Cut-Rate in downtown Piedmont. Hotels, theaters, and other public buildings and places fell under the Jim Crow laws, also known as the Black Codes. These laws, passed after Reconstruction in the 1880s, mandated segregation—separate areas in public places for blacks and whites, and did not allow the two groups to mingle. Public rest rooms were also off limits to "colored" people, as were department store dressing rooms. All public facilities—libraries, parks, and public transportation—were segregated. Blacks living in Piedmont were restricted in other ways. For example, African Americans could not own property in town until 1970. It wasn't until Henry was in college that his parents purchased a house.

The Irish and Italians held the highest paying jobs at the Westvaco Paper Mill. Moreover, only whites could belong to the labor unions, which weren't integrated until 1968. Most of the mill's black employees, including Henry's father, worked as loaders on the shipping platform. The loaders worked six days a week stacking paper into the trucks that transported Piedmont's main economic resource to the rest of the United States. Blacks and whites were not allowed to work side-by-side at the paper mill, nor were they allowed to socialize. Even the Westvaco Paper Mill's company picnics were segregated until the Civil Rights Act of 1964 was passed.

ALL IN THE FAMILY

In 1994, Henry Louis Gates, Jr. wrote *Colored People: A Memoir* in which he told of his childhood and what life was like for his parents, relatives, and neighbors in the town of Piedmont during segregation. Henry recalls that, like his father, his relatives on his mother's side, the Colemans, also worked as loaders at the Westvaco Paper Mill. Henry's maternal grandmother, "Big Mom," whom Henry referred to as "Biggie" was the head of the family. The authority figure of the Coleman clan, she was also a deeply spiritual woman. "She prayed a lot, and she never went anywhere . . . except to the doctor and to church," Henry remembers. She lived in a green house on the highest point "up on the hill" and Henry, who visited his grandmother often, genuinely liked her. The affection was reciprocated; Big Mom

Young Henry quickly became known by the affectionate nickname, "Skipper," a name he was called by his maternal grandmother, who was called "Big Mom," or "Biggie" by Henry. Gates still goes by the nickname "Skip" to this day.

called Henry "Skippy" and sometimes she called him "Skipper Dipper Ripper."

Big Mom and "Daddy Paul," Henry's maternal grandfather, had 12 living children—nine sons and three daughters. Daddy Paul worked as a handyman and a janitor, but Henry never knew his grandfather, who died five years before he was born. Skippy grew up encircled by the huge extended Coleman family. Christmas at Big Mom's and the annual Coleman family reunion on the last Sunday in July are just two happy memories from his childhood.

The Colemans were a virtuous family. Henry's Coleman aunts and uncles neither smoked, nor drank, nor gambled. They counted clean Christian living and traditional family values among their assets. They were also the last generation of Henry's family to live in "cradle to grave" segregation. Once integration came to the Westvaco Paper Mill, the Colemans came off the loading docks and advanced within the company.

Henry's relatives on his father's side of the family were as distant as the Colemans were close. The Gates family lived in Cumberland, Maryland, about 25 miles outside of Piedmont. The only time Henry recalls seeing all the members of his father's family together in one place was at his grandparents' funerals. Since they were the only times the Gates family gathered together, they served a dual role, doubling as family reunions. The Gateses lived a more casual lifestyle and did not embrace social taboos the way the Colemans did. The Colemans looked askance at the members of the Gates family, who tended to be free-thinkers and to pass the time telling stories. The Gateses also loved to dance to the bands of Duke Ellington and Cab Calloway at the Crystal Palace Ballroom in Cumberland, where there were special midnight shows for the blacks.

Henry can trace his father's family back before the Civil War, when his ancestors were enslaved people owned by a man named Horatio Gates. Gates held land in what is now Berkeley Springs, West Virginia, a town known for its mineral springs and spas. Henry's paternal grandfather, "Pop Gates," was the descendent of Jane Gates, born in 1816. It is believed that all of Jane's children were fathered by her white owner, an Irishman with the last name of Brady, who owned property outside of Cumberland, Maryland. Sometime during the 1860s, Brady gave Jane a large parcel of land in western Maryland. Part of the land became the 200-acre family farm at Patterson's Creek in West Virginia. Gates Point, the highest point in Mineral County, West Virginia, is located at Patterson's Creek.

Pop Gates's father, Edward, was Jane's oldest son. Edward married a woman named Maude Fortune. An educated woman who loved to read, Maude desired formal education for her three daughters, but insisted that Henry's grandfather stay at the farm and run it. Although the land remained in the Gates family until the 1920s, Maude and Henry moved off the farm and into a house on Greene Street in Cumberland in 1882. Pop Gates then went into business with his father, stoking chimneys and cleaning offices. Maude founded St. Phillip's Episcopal Church in Cumberland in 1890 and recruited priests from Haiti and Jamaica to serve as rectors. In 1919, Maude became a socialist (one who embraces Communism) and began to follow the teachings of the Communist leaders Karl Marx and Vladimir Lenin.

Pop Gates was light-skinned like his father. Pop Gates and his wife, Gertrude Helen Redman Gates, had seven sons, the youngest of whom was Henry's father, Henry Sr. He married Pauline Augusta Coleman, a seamstress who left high school so she could earn money to help her parents put her four brothers through college.

Henry Sr. and Pauline had two sons. Their eldest, Paul Edward, who was nicknamed "Rocky" after a character in a book, was born in 1945. A second son, born five years later, was named Louis Smith Gates. The Smith part of his name had an unusual origin. Pauline had promised an unmarried girlfriend that she would name her second son after her. "I had hated that name, Smith, felt deprived of my birthright. Finally I got around to telling my parents," Henry writes in

Henry's parents, Henry Sr. and Pauline, had two children. Their eldest son and Henry's older brother, Paul Edward, is today a prominent oral surgeon and chairperson of the Department of Dentistry at Bronx Lebanon Hospital in New York City. Pictured here, left to right, are Henry, Pauline, Henry Sr., and Paul Edward Gates.

his memoirs. Before his marriage in 1979, he legally changed his name to Henry Louis Gates, the name of his father.

At the time Henry was born, the Gates family was living in three tiny rooms. Henry's arrival further crowded the family, so in the evenings when it was time to go to bed, Rocky, who had been an only child for five years, was sent to the green house "up the hill," to sleep at Big Mom's. When Henry was four years old, his family moved to Pearl Street and rented a house owned by Doctor Woverton. As

Pauline sat in the kitchen sewing, little Henry would play with puppets, marionettes, or the "Betsy McCall" paper dolls that came with *McCall's* magazine. It was here, in the kitchen, that Pauline taught her youngest son to read and write before he entered first grade.

Henry's brother, Rocky, now uses his given name, Paul Edward Gates. He is a prominent oral surgeon and chairperson of the Department of Dentistry at Bronx Lebanon Hospital in New York City. He recalls the importance of family during his and his brother's childhood:

> There was little poverty in Piedmont. We thought of ourselves as middle class and we didn't want for anything. Piedmont was a safe and warm environment where we were surrounded by a tremendous extended family. Our relatives even worked at the mill. My mother was one of thirteen children, and the majority of her siblings lived within five miles of their mother, our grandmother. There were always relatives looking out for us.

TELEVISION: WINDOW TO THE WORLD

Although Piedmont neighborhoods were divided by race and ethnicity, occasional mixing of the races was inevitable. Henry encountered white people in downtown Piedmont, at the bank, or while shopping. His first introduction to the white world, however, came from television. His favorite shows were *The Life of Riley, Ozzie and Harriet,* and *Leave it to Beaver.* "These shows for us were about property, the property that white people could own and that we couldn't. About a level of comfort and ease at which we could only wonder," recalled Henry.

If watching white people on television was fascinating

for young Henry, seeing black people starring in their own television shows was even more enthralling. In the 1950s, there were no black news anchors or talk show hosts like Oprah Winfrey. "Colored, colored on channel two," Henry's neighbors would shout from their front porches to alert all within ear shot that a show featuring black people was being shown on television. One of the Gates family's favorite shows was *Amos and Andy*. "What was special to us about *Amos and Andy* was that their world was *all* colored, just like ours. Of course, *they* had their colored judges and lawyers and doctors and nurses, which we could only dream about having, or becoming—and we *did* dream about those things."

In addition to providing entertainment, the television was a lifeline that brought the events of the rest of the country home to Piedmont, West Virginia. Around the time Henry was preparing to enter school in the mid-1950s, America was undergoing great social and political change. Blacks and whites alike were fighting for the civil rights of all Americans and were bringing the injustices of racism and segregation to the forefront of public awareness. In 1955, in Montgomery, Alabama, a young black seamstress named Rosa Parks refused to give up her seat to a white man on a segregated bus. Her arrest sparked the Montgomery Bus Boycott, which was led by a young Birmingham, Alabama, minister named Dr. Martin Luther King, Jr. King urged nonviolent means of bringing about change. In 1964, the United States Congress passed the Civil Rights Act, making it a federal offense for any state to continue the practice of segregation.

The change from a segregated to an integrated society was difficult for some states. The people of Little Rock, Arkansas, fought desegregation and refused to allow five black students to attend Little Rock High School. Each school day, the black students were escorted into the high school by Arkansas national guardsmen. The year was 1957, and Henry was in the second grade. Like African Americans throughout the country, the entire black community of Piedmont turned to television to watch the events unfolding in Little Rock. "We watched it on TV," Henry recalled. "All of us watched it. I don't mean Mama and Daddy and Rocky. I mean *all* the colored people in America watched it, together, with one set of eyes. We'd watch it in the morning . . . before we'd go to school; we'd watch it in the evening, on the news . . . We'd watch the special bulletins at night, interrupting our TV shows."

INTEGRATION

Once it became clear that Piedmont, like the rest of America, was going to become an integrated society, Pauline and Henry wanted to be a part of the community. In 1957, Pauline became the first black secretary of the Parent Teacher Association in Piedmont. Henry remembers with pride the way his mother, wearing her fanciest dress, would stand at the podium and read the PTA minutes. "Both our mother and our father were considered the black liaisons to the white community. [Either one or the other was] involved in politics, the United Way, or school and sports events," remembers Paul Gates.

Social implications aside, Pauline Gates saw little personal advantage in integration because she never liked white people. Her opinion of whites had been influenced by her experiences as a young girl working in Piedmont as a servant for wealthy white people, who had been unkind to her. The benefit of an integrated world to her sons, however, was not lost upon her. Henry remembers:

But she wanted us to go to integrated schools. She wanted us to live in an integrated economy. She wanted us even to live in integrated neighborhoods. She wanted us to be able to get the best that American society offered. She wanted us to be articulate . . . You know, she wanted us to know how to dress, how to talk, how to act, how to behave. She wanted us to go to private schools, to the Ivy League. I mean, she wanted us to be as successful as it was humanly possible to be in American society. But she always wanted us to remember, first and last, that we were black and that you could never trust white people.

3

Setting Out for Elsewhere

"Overachiever designated a sort of pathology; the overstraining of your natural capacity."

—Henry Louis Gates, Jr.,
Colored People: A Memoir

"Piedmont was set in its ways and slow to change, and although civil rights took us all by surprise, the town was not beset by the riots and violence that affected other cities as the Civil Rights Act began to take affect," recalls Gates. When integration did come to the town, the schools were among the first to feel the impact. The town's only elementary school, the Davis Free School, had been founded in 1906. The three-story red brick building sat at the top of Kenny House Hill, its six grades educating 250 students. After *Brown* v. *Board of Education* was decided by the Supreme Court, Davis Free School quietly integrated in 1955, the year before Henry was to start. His firsthand experiences at the forefront of integration would become a common subject of his writing in later years.

The push to desegregate American public schools began in the city of Topeka, Kansas, in 1951, when Oliver Brown, the black father of a third grade student, sued the Topeka Board of Education to allow his daughter to attend a whites-only school. Brown's daughter, Linda, had to walk one mile through a dangerous railroad switchyard and cross a busy intersection to catch a bus to take her to the all-black Monroe School, even though there was a white elementary school a few blocks from where she lived. When Brown attempted to enroll Linda in the nearby school, its principal refused to accept his daughter's application. Brown then approached McKinley Burnett, the head of Topeka's branch of the National Association for the Advancement of Colored People (NAACP) and asked for assistance.

The NAACP had long wanted to confront segregation in public schools, and force public officials to uphold the Fourteenth Amendment, which had been ratified in 1868. The Fourteenth Amendment guaranteed equal rights for all with the words: " . . . nor shall any State deprive any person of life, liberty or property, without due process of law; nor deny to any person within its jurisdiction the equal protection of the law." Yet, at the same time, laws enforced separate schools for black children and white children, as long as the schools for blacks were educationally equal to the schools for whites.

A LANDMARK CASE

In 1951, the NAACP appeared before the U.S. District Court for Kansas to request a ruling that would desegregate Topeka's public schools. The NAACP argued that segregated schools made black children feel inferior to white children and presented psychological research that stated:

> . . . Segregation of white and colored children in public schools has a detrimental effect upon the colored children. The impact is greater when it has the sanction of the law, for the policy of separating the races is usually interpreted as denoting the inferiority of the Negro group. A sense of inferiority affects the motivation of a child to learn. Segregation with the sanction of law, therefore, has a tendency to retard the educational and mental development of Negro children and to deprive them of some of the benefits they would receive in a racially integrated school system.

In its defense, the Topeka Board of Education cited accomplished African Americans, such as Frederick Douglass and Booker T. Washington, who had lived in a segregated society and gone on to make successful contributions. The Topeka Board of Education also argued that because America was a segregated society, segregated schools could be viewed as preparation for the lifelong segregation black children would face.

In reaching its decision, the Kansas District Court studied *Plessey* v. *Ferguson*, a court case from 1896 that found constitutional reasons for a separate but equal educational system for blacks and whites. Since *Plessey* v. *Ferguson* had never been overturned, the Kansas District Court ruled in favor of the Topeka Board of Education.

On October 1, 1951, Brown and the NAACP took their case to the U.S. Supreme Court. By then school segregation was being challenged in other states, and the Kansas case was combined with other similar legal proceedings. The Supreme Court failed to reach a decision when it heard the case for the first time on December 9, 1952. When the case was presented for the second time, on December 7–8, 1953, the Court requested both sides study "the circumstances surrounding the adoption of the Fourteenth Amendment in 1868" to determine if the separate but equal clause also included schools.

On May 17, 1954, the Supreme Court unanimously agreed that segregation of children in public schools solely on the basis of race, even though the physical facilities and other tangible factors may be equal, deprives the children of the minority group equal educational opportunities. The Supreme Court justices also found that in the field of public education, the doctrine of "separate but equal" has no place and that separate educational facilities are inherently unequal and deprive those forced to attend them of the equal protection of the laws guaranteed by the Fourteenth Amendment.

Ultimately, the Supreme Court justices determined that their decision would rest on whether segregated schools deprived black children of equal protection of the law. When the justices ruled that it did, schools across America were ordered to desegregate.

The Board of Education of West Virginia's Mineral County, in which the town of Piedmont was located, responded rapidly to the Supreme Court's decision to outlaw segregated schools. Howard High School, the high school for blacks, was closed. "There wasn't enough money to support two high schools in a town as small as Piedmont," explained Paul Gates. After living segregated lifestyles and studying in segregated schools, Piedmont's young people found themselves in uncharted waters. A new set of rules was quickly established for the integrated school system, which Henry entered in 1956. There could be no interracial dating, dancing, or holding hands. The number of blacks on the starting line of the football team was sharply limited, and there could be no more than one black cheerleader. The principal of the closed black high school became the sole black teacher in the integrated high school.

"Everyone I knew was excited about integration, and everyone was scared," said Henry. The older students were especially affected, and many experienced culture shock after so many years of attending segregated schools. Even so, Paul Gates, who attended segregated schools until sixth grade, called the integration of the Piedmont schools "seamless." Integration happened so quickly in the Piedmont school system that it took the rest of Piedmont several years to catch up.

STRIVING FOR SUCCESS

In the midst of the social change swirling around him, Henry grew into a personable boy who got along with others. "Everyone loved Skip," remembers Paul Gates. "He was a warm child who was always smiling." As a youngster, Henry loved photography and kept photo albums of the pictures he took.

Determined to follow in the academic footsteps of his brother, Henry set a course of academic achievement for himself from his very first day at school. "I was quiet, I was smart, I had a good memory, I already knew how to read and write, and I was blessed with the belief that I could learn anything," Henry wrote in *Colored People: A Memior*. Encouraged by his teachers, Henry showed academic promise early on. In the second grade, he scored 489 correct answers out of 500 on a standardized test. Both Rocky and Henry scored such high marks on standardized intelligence tests that a teacher came to their home to personally give Pauline and Henry Sr. their sons' scores.

One of the most significant events influencing Henry's elementary school education involved not himself, but Rocky. Annually, the state of West Virginia awarded the Golden Horseshoe, a prestigious award for excellence in history, to four eighth grade students from each county. The year Rocky was in eighth-grade, he was legally one of the champions from Mineral County and the first black student to be eligible for the award. However, he was passed up for the prize because the hotel in the state capital, Charleston, where the winners were staying, was segregated. To cover up their inability to give the award to Rocky, the judges on the county school board lied and told him he had lost the prize because he had misspelled a word.

"Something happened to Rocky when that county school board lied and told him that he had almost won," wrote Gates. ". . . I saw him nursing the injury in silence, unable to speak of it, unwilling to shed it . . . the knowledge of that deception cast a shadow over his life."

Henry was determined to follow in his brother's footsteps, and six years after Rocky had been passed over for the award, Henry was one of the Golden Horseshoe winners of his eighth-grade class.

Henry never forgot the injustice Rocky endured. On his brother's 35th birthday, Henry arranged for him to receive his long-overdue Golden Horseshoe, which was presented to him with an apology from the governor of West Virginia.

Eight years later, the *Charleston Gazette* of West Virginia named Paul Gates "West Virginian of the Year," and the West Virginian state legislature passed an act that once again recognized Paul Gates's rightful earning of the Golden Horseshoe. For a second time, Henry acknowledged the important role his older brother had played in his life.

FATHER AND SON

Although Henry developed a close bond with his mother early on, he didn't form a close relationship with his father until he was 12 years old. Henry had enormous admiration for his mother, and it was from her that he acquired his sense of self-respect. "As a child, I was secure in her knowledge of things, of how to do things and function in the world, of how to be in the world and command respect. In her courage I was safe," Henry has said of his mother.

Pauline contributed to the household income by cleaning homes, and Henry Sr. worked two jobs six days a week. He would return home after working at his job as a loader at the Westvaco Paper Mill, eat a quick supper with his family, and then dash off to his second job as a janitor at the local telephone company. When he was not working, Henry Sr. would read, work on crossword puzzles, or watch television. Henry Sr. was also a big sports fan, and he and his sons often traveled to Pittsburgh, Pennsylvania, to attend sporting events at Forbes Field. "My mother didn't care for sports, so she rarely came with us," said Paul Gates.

To Henry, it seemed that Rocky was the favorite son. Rocky was built like an athlete, and he and Henry Sr. bonded over sports, especially baseball. Rocky was "tall, lean, and handsome, blessed with my father's metabolism," wrote Henry. Rocky was also the first black captain of the basketball team at the high school, for which he would be the first black to awarded a commemorative wristwatch at graduation.

Unlike Rocky, who loved to be involved in sports, Henry would rather read about sports than participate in them, although he did serve one short, unsuccessful season of little league as a catcher. Henry Sr. was openly critical of Henry, often opposing his opinions, embarrassing him by correcting him in front of strangers. ". . . Pop and I had some hard times. He thought that I didn't love him, and I thought he didn't love me. At times, we both were right," Henry wrote in *Colored People: A Memior*.

"We grew up in a town where an African-American male was distinguished by his athletic ability or his ability to hunt, and even to some extent, his womanizing. Skippy's physique may have kept him away from athletics, but he found other ways to establish himself; he became an excellent scorekeeper for the baseball team, for example," remembers Paul Gates.

Henry's lack of exercise took its toll, and as a child he had to wear husky-sized clothing. Henry's father and brother teased him about his weight, calling him "Two-Ton Tony Galento" and "Chicken Flinsterwall." Henry's classmates made fun of him and called him "Hoss Cartwright," after the heavyset character in *Bonanza*, a popular television show at the time. "I was short and round—not obese, mind you, but *fat*. Still, I was clean and energetic, and most of the time I was cheerful. And I liked to play with other kids, not so much because I enjoyed the things we did together but because I could watch them be happy." Henry also had flat feet. To build up his arches, he wore corrective shoes, which he detested.

Henry's first experiences with multiculturalism started right in his own town. Because of his passion for sports, Henry Sr. became somewhat of a substitute father to his sons' friends, including Italian and Irish children. Despite this familiarity, however, the social interaction had limits. Although Henry's friends were often at his home, they never stayed for dinner; nor were they invited to sleep overnight. Likewise, Henry was never invited to dinner or to sleep at their homes.

Henry's favorite subjects in school were geography and history, yet he was planning a career in either medicine or law. When he was in sixth grade, Henry was the smartest student in the class. When he was in seventh grade, he was advanced a year in several subjects. He began reading serious books at that time, and spent Saturdays at the public library in the nearby town of Keyser. He would borrow audio recordings of Shakespeare, which he listened to as he read the plays. As a teenager, he enjoyed listening to rhythm and blues music and Nat King Cole, Johnny Mathias, and John R, a white southerner who sang gospel and soul. Henry read books by the African-American authors Eldridge Cleaver and Ralph Ellison. He was popular with his classmates, who elected him class president several times.

THE CROSSROADS OF CHILDHOOD

As he neared his teenage years, Henry came face to face with two life-changing experiences. The first occurred when he was 12 years old. His mother, who was 46, experienced a severe depressive disorder, which may have been caused by menopause. Of this time in his life, Henry wrote ". . . it was beyond my comprehension. I only knew that something had eclipsed the woman who gave birth to me and raised me, and that nothing I could do seemed to restore things. I was powerless, and so was she. . . . Mama's 'change' was the great crisis in my life, the crossroads of my childhood. I was devastated."

Henry believed he had caused Pauline's illness, and when her condition forced her to be hospitalized, Henry prayed that she would survive and promised to give his life to the church if she did. He joined Big Mom's church, the Walden Methodist Church, and for the next two years, he stopped going to dances and playing cards. He spent a lot of time in church, praying, and reading his Bible.

The summer he was 13, Henry felt a sharp pain in his knee while playing touch football. The pain would not subside, even after Henry treated it with liniment, exercise, and rest. Seeking relief, he saw several doctors who couldn't agree on a diagnosis. One doctor thought he had pulled a muscle and gave him a cane. Another doctor thought he had pulled a ligament and gave him a pair of crutches. It wasn't until September, when he was back in school, that his real problem, a hairline fracture of his hip joint, was discovered. The medical term for his condition is "slipped epithesis," and it was treated by putting Henry's leg in a cast. The doctor applying the cast asked Henry about his studies as he treated him. Henry relates the conversation in his memoir:

> Boy, he said, I understand you want to be a doctor.
> Yessir. You always said 'sir' to white people—unless you were trying to make a statement.
> Had I taken a lot of science courses? He wanted to know.
> I said, Yessir, I enjoy science.
> Are you good at it?
> Yessir, I believe so.
> He said, Tell me, who was the father of sterilization?
> Joseph Lister.
> Then he asked who discovered penicillin.

Alexander Fleming, I answered.

And what about DNA?

Watson and Crick.

The interview went on like this. I thought my answers might get me a pat on the head. Actually, they just confirmed a medical judgment he'd come to.

The doctor diagnosed Henry's hip problem as psycho-somatic and told Henry's mother his pain was caused by his desire to overachieve. The doctor's definition of ". . . overachiever designated a sort of pathology; the over-straining of your natural capacity," Gates was to say many years later.

The racist attitude of the doctor delayed the correct diagnosis, and the result was a permanent hip injury. Henry's irate mother transferred him to the University Medical Center in Morgantown, which was 60 miles away. The following year, Henry had three operations on his hip. He lost time from school, and although he was able to keep up with most of his subjects, he fell behind in geometry after the first surgery. By the time he caught up, he had to be hospitalized again. The steel pins that had been intro-duced into his hip during the first operation had failed. A second surgery removed the pins and a third surgery, a cup arthroplasty (the insertion of a metal ball in his hip joint), followed.

Henry was immobilized for the next six weeks and was confined to bed in traction with a series of pulleys and weights. He was unable to move his body—unable to sit up, turnover, or get up to use the bathroom. Throughout his confinement, his mother stayed with him in the hospital from morning until night. She had rented a small room in a nearby hotel that catered to the family members of patients. By then her depression was starting to subside and focusing on her son seemed to lift it even more. Henry recalls this time with his mother in his memoirs:

> I spent my time quarreling with her . . . Every day . . . I'd insist she go back to Piedmont—or she would insist that she was going back to Piedmont. I think we both came to realize that this was a sort of ritual. I didn't like being a patient, and stoicism wasn't my strong suit. We'd argue about anything and everything—even about what time of day it was—but the arguments kept me from thinking about that traction system. And maybe they helped her escape her own darkening obsessions.

Eventually, Henry learned to walk again, but when he was released from the hospital, it was with crutches. The operation had left his right leg shorter than his left, and he was forced, once again, to wear the dreaded orthopedic shoes, this time with a lift in the right heel.

Paul Gates remembers: "I'm sure there were times when Skippy felt depressed, but [the disability] did not stop him. I was in college by then, but I don't ever remember him feeling sorry for himself."

Looking back on the racist attitude of the doctor, Henry said that "The most subtle and pernicious form of racism against blacks [is] doubt over our intellectual capacities." Throughout his life, Henry has fought, and won his personal battle with racism through scholarship and academic excellence.

THE WORLD OUTSIDE OF PIEDMONT

While Henry was a patient at the University Medical Center, Father Smith, an Episcopal priest from Keyser, visited him. By then, Henry had decided he no longer wished to be a part of Walden Methodist Church. His mother's recovery, he felt, freed him from the promise he had made to the church, and he had been growing disenchanted with religion. "I had been tiring of . . . the Methodist Church. It was as if I had outgrown a good pair of trousers, my favorite trousers, and had no others to put on. I wanted to learn how to be a free Negro and to be a man, how to be in the world and with God, how to question values and tradition without being kicked out of the fold, how to value community and order, family and the group, yet not have to suppress my uncertainties, doubts, ambivalences in order to be accepted. . . . Father Smith seemed to understand all this."

For the next three summers, encouraged by his uncle Harry, a Methodist minister, Henry attended Peterkin, an Episcopal church camp in the Allegheny Mountains of West Virginia. Scholarships funded his stays, which proved to be double opportunities for Henry. Not only was he becoming acquainted with a new faith, for the first time he was experiencing the world outside of his hometown. He was one of three black teenagers who attended the camp.

For two weeks each summer, Henry lived with more than 100 other teenagers who, like him, were questioning all aspects of their lives. ". . . we'd talk about this and that and everything, books and ideas, people and concepts. The war in Vietnam. Smoking. The existence of God.... We drank ideas and ate controversy. . . . Can you love two people at the same time? I feasted on the ideas of learning about the world and being a citizen of it." While at Peterkin Camp, Henry read the work of African-American writer James Baldwin for the first time and devoured his writings. He copied passages from the author's books into his diary and soon was trying to model Baldwin's writing style. According to Henry, Baldwin ". . . determined the direction of my intellectual life more than did any other single factor. . . . His prose shaped my identity as an Afro-American, as much by the questions he raised as by the answers he provided."

The first summer Henry spent at Peterkin, the Watts race riots in Los Angeles made the headlines. The year before, in 1964, the Civil Rights Act had been passed. In response, California had passed an act which would block fair housing in the state. Disenfranchised blacks, many who lived in poverty in the inner cities, rose up in protest. The Watts section of south central Los Angeles was one such area. During the riots, the residents not only protested unfair housing, but also a high inner-city unemployment rate and poor schools. On August 11, 1965, six days of rioting broke out, killing 34 people, injuring over 1,000, and causing over $200 million in property damage. Approximately 4,000 people were arrested.

When news of the riots reached Peterkin, Henry's first reaction was bewilderment. "I didn't understand what a riot was. Were colored people being killed by white people, or were they killing white people? . . . I experienced that strange combination of power and powerlessness that you feel when the actions of another black person affect your own life, simply because you both are black. I realized that the actions of people I did not know had become my responsibility as surely as if the black folk in Watts had been my relatives in Piedmont, just 20 or so miles away."

Once back home, guided by Father Smith and the enlightening experience of attending Peterkin summer camp, Henry officially broke away from Walden Methodist

Church and joined Father Smith's Episcopal Church in Keyser. Although his mother had been a devout Methodist, his father had been Episcopalian from the time his grandmother, Maude, had founded St. Phillip's Episcopal Church in the late 1800s. Henry's mother joined the Episcopalian church with Henry, and for the first time, the family began regularly attending church together.

As he was recovering from surgery, Henry briefly attended Exeter, a private preparatory school in Devon, England. The cold climate, however, irritated his hip, and Henry returned to Piedmont High School, where his excellent grades made him the valedictorian and gave him the opportunity to speak at his high school graduation in 1968. School policy forbade presenting an unauthorized speech, but Henry secretly wrote a second valedictory on controversial subjects like the Vietnam War, civil rights, and abortion. Each day he practiced the traditional speech with his teacher at school, then came home, and rehearsed his own speech in the evenings with his mother, who had always encouraged her sons to be independent thinkers. "My speech was . . . about the individual's rights and responsibilities in his or her community, and about the necessity to defy norms out of love," Henry wrote.

The next fall found Henry preparing for a career as a physician at Potomac State College of West Virginia University, five miles away in Keyser. Says his brother, "Skip never thought anything would be impossible to achieve. He was very entrepreneurial; he had a plan and he knew that to go where he wanted to go, he would have to leave Piedmont, have to leave West Virginia. The summers he spent at Peterkin and the brief time at Exeter had exposed him to people and experiences he had never before known, and he would always come back from other places enthusiastic and full of life." To Henry, living as he did in a small town the size of Piedmont, the world was made up of two places: the Valley and Elsewhere. Henry knew he would find himself Elsewhere. He planned to go to the University of West Virginia's main campus in Morgantown after he graduated Potomac State, then on to medical school at Harvard or Yale. An inspirational college professor, however, coupled with a love of literature, were soon to change Henry's mind about a career as a doctor.

4

Of African Descent, But Not From Africa

> "Reading books was something I always thought of as a pastime, certainly not as a vocation. 'The Duke' [Duke Anthony Whitmore] made the study of literature an alluring prospect."
>
> —Henry Louis Gates, Jr.,
> *Colored People: A Memoir*

Most people from the Potomac Valley who attended college began by studying at Potomac State Junior College in nearby Keyser. Rocky had started there before continuing at West Virginia University to study for his doctorate of dental surgery degree. Both Gates sons also began their college careers with a heaping dose of self-confidence spooned out by their mother. "She reinforced over and over and over again that, in her opinion, we were beautiful and brilliant. . . . I don't know if any of those things were true, but if someone says it to you every day . . . you become hypnotized by that. . . . My mother bred a tremendous amount of intellectual self-confidence in my brother and me."

Henry had heard a lot about Potomac State from his cousin, Greg, who studied there. Greg was especially eager for Henry to meet one of his English professors, Duke Anthony Whitmore. "There's an English teacher down there, who's going to blow your mind," Greg told Henry. Whitmore reawakened in Henry a passion for English and American literature, and Henry says meeting him was the beginning of the end of his 12-year dream of becoming a doctor.

"Learning English and American literature from the Duke was a game to which I looked forward to every day. I had always loved English and had been blessed with some dedicated and able teachers. But reading books was something I had always thought of as a pastime, certainly not as a vocation. The Duke made the study of literature an alluring prospect."

In his memoir, Gates writes that "It was a glorious experience. Words and thoughts, ideas and visions, came alive for me in his [Whitmore's] classroom. It was he who showed me, by his example, that ideas had a life of their own and that there were other professions as stimulating and as rewarding as being a doctor."

Professor Whitmore encouraged Henry to continue his education at an Ivy League school after his freshman year at Potomac State. Gates applied to Yale University. To earn money for college, he took a summer job recruiting blacks for the integrated labor unions at the Westvaco Paper Mill.

Once at Yale, Gates began to consider pursuing a law degree, and he majored in American political history. He enrolled in a program called the "Five Year B.A.," which allowed students to take a year's leave from their studies to pursue nonacademic interests. Gates wanted to use the year to travel to Africa. He had been fascinated with the continent since 1960, when several African nations had won independence. At that time, as a 10-year-old boy, he had memorized the names of each African country, its capital, and its leader, mimicking the way the television anchor pronounced them on the evening news.

TO AFRICA AND BACK

In 1970, Gates traveled to Tanzania. For one year, he worked helping to administer anesthesia in an Anglican mission hospital in Kilimatinde. His experiences in Tanzania included living among the Wagogo villagers and peasants, and the Masai herdsmen. "My very first night was spent in tears, wondering what could have possessed me to pledge to live in a village of 500 people with no electricity, telephones, television, or running water, and where the 'express' bus (which delivered both telegrams and the mail) passed through just twice each week," he wrote.

On this, the first of many trips to Africa, Gates learned that "I was of African descent, but not from Africa." On his way home, Gates and a recent Harvard graduate, Lawrence Biddle Weeks, traveled from the Indian Ocean to the Atlantic Ocean without ever leaving the ground. Mostly hitchhiking, the two men began their journey in Dar es Salaam, the capital of Tanzania, and traveled north to Mombassa, Kenya. From there, they went on to Kenya's capital, Nairobi, then continued into Kampala, Uganda. They arrived in Uganda a day after the dictator Idi Amin's 1971 coup. On the final leg of the trip, Gates and Weeks traveled to the city of Kisangani, the major port of the Congo River, then finally to Kinshasha in the Democratic

Republic of the Congo. The trip took over two months, and although it was an exciting adventure, Gates became sick from dysentery and lost almost 30 pounds.

On the return trip home, Gates wrote to John David Rockefeller IV, the West Virginia secretary of state who was running for governor, and asked him for a summer job working on his campaign. During the summer before his junior year at Yale, Gates returned to West Virginia and worked in Charleston for Rockefeller. Although Rockefeller's 1972 bid for governor was unsuccessful, he did go on to win the governorship in 1976 and was reelected in 1980. Rockefeller was later elected to the United States Senate in 1984, where he served the people of West Virginia. It was while working on the 1972 campaign that Gates met his future wife, a white campaign worker named Sharon Adams. The two were married seven years later, on September 1, 1979, and had two daughters, Maggie and Liza.

WRITING AND LITERATURE

In September of 1971, Gates returned to Yale. The following year, he applied to become a Yale Scholar of the House, a prestigious honor that allows a student to work on a project of his choosing instead of attending classes. Each year, Yale chose 12 outstanding students to be Scholars of the House. Gates was selected, and he spent his senior year writing *The Once and Future King*, a book that he never published. The book chronicled Rockefeller's unsuccessful bid for office. The book so impressed John Morton Blum, Gates's Yale advisor and professor, that he told Gates he could either be an academic or a journalist. Professor Blum encouraged Gates to become a writer. "I learned a lot about writing from John Blum and I learned a lot of history from John Blum," Gates told National Endowment for the

Humanities Chairmen, Bruce Cole, after being selected to present the 2002 Jefferson Lecture in Humanities.

By the time he was a senior at Yale, Gates's writing had already begun to earn praise on the college campus. When he returned to school after his year in Africa, Gates became a guest columnist for the college's daily paper, the *Yale Daily News*, when an editor asked him to write about his experiences at the missionary hospital in Tanzania.

Gates spent many hours in the university's libraries, in particular at the Beinecke Rare Book Library, where he studied the James Weldon Johnson archives of African-American arts and letters. In the early 1970s, the discipline of African-American Studies was still in its infancy and in the process of differentiating itself from the academic disciplines of sociology and anthropology. After writing a paper on Bessie Smith, a blues singer, one of Gates's professors remarked that the paper demonstrated the type of archival research combined with individual interpretation and understanding that was needed in the new academic discipline of African-American Studies.

"I realized that if I could combine my love for archival work and . . . theoretical developments . . . that maybe I could make a contribution to both the study of literature . . . and to a nascent field which was perilously close to dying, called Afro-American Studies," Gates recalled.

After graduating summa cum laude from Yale in 1973 with a B.A. in history, Gates left for England. He had received a Mellon Fellowship to continue his studies at Clare College, Cambridge University. This award had never before been presented to an African American. Once his education plans were in place, Gates wrote to an editor at *Time* magazine, enclosing some of his *Yale Daily News* columns, and asked for a job as a correspondent from England. The promise of employment secured, Gates sailed for Southampton, England on the Queen Elizabeth II. Eventually he became *Time* magazine's London Bureau Staff correspondent.

Gates was expecting to continue his studies of history at Clare College, so he was surprised at his unexpected attachment to English literature. At first Gates found it difficult to make the transition to a new academic interest. He remembers:

> [When I arrived at Cambridge] I didn't even know what literary theory was. When I wrote my first essay, my supervisor said it was the worst essay she had ever read, because I didn't know how to explicate a text. I went to her and I said, 'Surely there must be books to teach me this method?' She said, 'No, no, you're born with it. It's some sort of sensibility that you get through your genes.' Well, being a practical American, I went to the bookstore and I asked for the literary criticism section and I bought it—the whole section. I bought one discrete title of each book, and I went back and I read those books and I ended up doing very well, Thank goodness.

RAINBOW COALITION OF MENTORS

While studying at Cambridge, Gates met Wole Soyinka, a Nigerian playwright who was a visiting professor. Soyinka was a political exile who had been imprisoned for over two years in Nigeria, much of that time in solitary confinement, for writings that protested the Biafran War. (The Republic of Biafra was a sucessionist state of West Africa that existed from 1967–1970.) He published a book about his imprisonment titled, *The Man Died*, and had to flee for his life to avoid further persecution.

Gates describes Soyinka as a "bushy-haired man who wore dashikis [brightly colored, loose-fitting garments]," who wanted to teach African literature at Cambridge University. Although Soyinka gave a series of lectures the first year that Gates attended, he was denied a full professorship. "[The administration at Cambridge] said African literature was, at best, sociology or socio-anthropology, but it was not real literature," Gates explained. It was Soyinka's lecture series, "Myth, Literature and the African World," that sparked Gates's interest in African and African-American literature. About 13 years later, in 1986, Soyinka would go on to become the first African to receive the Nobel Prize in Literature.

Also while a student at Cambridge, Gates met Kwame Anthony Appiah, a student from Ghana. Gates and Appiah developed a close friendship, and Appiah later joined Gates at Yale University. Appiah would eventually find his way to Harvard University and become the Charles H. Carswell Professor of Afro-American Studies and of Philosophy. Later he would be appointed the Laurance S. Rockefeller University Professor of Philosophy at the University Center for Human Values at Princeton University. Over the years, Gates and Appiah worked on several projects together, including *Encarta Africana*, a complete collection of information about black history and culture in Africa, the Americas, Europe, and the Caribbean.

Of his two colleagues, Soyinka and Appiah, Gates has said: "Much of my passion for African Studies was generated by Soyinka's . . . example, and it is clear to me today that had it not been for our chance encounter, and my deep friendship with . . . Kwame Anthony Appiah, I would have ended up neither as a professor nor as a scholar of African or African-American Studies."

African-American Studies allow for the examination of people of African descent, including Americans, Caribbeans, and Latin Americans, from a historical, cultural, political, and sociological perspective. The call for institutions of higher learning to offer such studies can be traced to the late 1800s, when educators such as Alexander Cromwell, Arthur Schomburg, and W.E.B. Du Bois founded the American Negro Academy. With the passage of the Civil Rights Act in 1964, the importance of studying the significance of African Americans in the history of America became apparent. By the early 1970s, centers of African-American Studies were being created in colleges and universities throughout the country.

Gates received a master of arts degree from Cambridge in 1974, then returned to New Haven to live while writing the dissertation for the doctorate degree that he would receive from Cambridge. To support himself, he became a public relations representative for the American Cyanamid Company.

From October 1, 1975 to June 30, 1976, Gates worked as a secretary in Yale University's Department of African-American Studies, then he served as a lecturer until he completed his doctoral thesis in 1979 in English language and literature. Gates became the first African American to receive a Ph.D. from Cambridge University in its 800-year history. After earning his doctorate, he joined the faculty at Yale as an assistant professor of both English and African-American Studies.

In addition to Wole Soyinka, the literary critic George Steiner, the Pulitzer Prize-winning historian William McFeeley, and the historian John Blassingame, became Gates's mentors. The group used to meet for breakfast every morning at a local pizzeria to discuss their research. Gates refers to the group as his "rainbow coalition of mentors."

Blassingame, who died in 2000, was known for his study of slaves. He was a former head of Yale's African-American Studies program and a special inspiration to Gates. Even after Gates had proved himself a true archivist and historian with his discovery of *Our Nig*, he continued to learn from Blassingame. In later years, as Gates worked to build the discipline of African-American Studies, Blassingame's ideas influenced Gates. ". . . [Blassingame] was very influential in shaping my understanding of the agenda for Afro-American Studies as we sought to move it from a feel-good politically based, ethnic cheerleading orientation to a real academic discipline."

Gates entered the world of academia with his essay, "Preface to Blackness: Text and Pretext" published in *Afro-American Literature: The Reconstruction of Instruction*. This, as well as other critical essays on African-American literature, won Gates a grant from the National Endowment for the Humanities in 1980. In 1981, the MacArthur Foundation honored him as one of 21 exceptional scholars, and awarded him a five-year grant of $150,000. One of the first projects on which Gates worked was The Black Periodical Literature Project, for which he researched and interpreted African-American periodicals and other literature, uncovering thousands of pieces of lost African-American writing. In 1981, while he was at Yale, Gates discovered Harriet E. Wilson's book, *Our Nig*. In 1984, Gates was appointed associate professor of English and undergraduate director for the Department of Afro-American Studies at Yale. That same year, his book, *Black Literature and Literary Theory*, was published. This book on black literary tradition and criticism sparked controversy in both literature and African-American studies circles.

5

Black Literary Theory

> "Literary theory functioned in my education as a prism, which I could turn to refract different spectral patterns of language use in a text, as one does with daylight. Turn the prism this way, and one pattern of color emerges; turn it that way, and another pattern configures . . ."
>
> —Henry Louis Gates, Jr., *Figures in Black: Works, Signs, and the "Racial" Self*

Literature can be defined as a body of written work created by people who are bound together by a common language or culture and produced during a specific time in history. Literature is a multi-faceted art form, and therefore can be viewed from many perspectives. In its most basic form, literature is a marriage of language and ideas, and one can neither write, nor read literature without experiencing the social, political, racial, gender, personal, and historical perspectives inherent in the writing. A body of literature generally considered of lasting importance is known as a *canon.*

For untold generations, literature has served to give meaning to the human condition and strengthen the bonds that connect people. An author's experiences, as told through literature, can influence and enrich the life of the reader. Literature gives shape and form to abstract thought while at the same time uses imagination to express detail. Because literature explores the relationship between cultural groups and the world as a whole, it offers an opportunity to study and understand different cultural and ethnic groups.

Literature also serves other purposes. It allows for the articulation and communication of similarities, as well as differences, between groups. As a means of expression, literature allows for self-definition by widening the range of social acceptability.

One of the purposes of literature is to provoke thought. A literary scholar is one who analyzes literature with the specific intent of interpreting it in the context of its differing perspectives. Literature studied in this manner is said to be explicated, or explained. Literary scholarship explores the different layers of a writing in an attempt to uncover the motivating factors that influenced the author and the message the author is trying to convey. In essence, when studying a particular piece of literature, a literary scholar searches for the expression of an author's meaning in the hope of guiding the reader to a greater appreciation of a piece of writing. At the same time, however, a literary scholar can help readers better understand their own spheres of influence by applying the past to the present and contrasting differences with similarities.

When a literary scholar commits interpretation of literature to the written word, the result is called literary criticism. There are many styles of contemporary literary criticism, and each arises from a specific body of texts. Formalism emphasizes the writer's writing techniques over the work's written structure. Structuralism takes into consideration the elements of the work's structures, while post-structuralism is a critical style that studies a work by taking it apart or dissecting it. The feminist and Marxist styles are two other forms of literary criticism.

GATES'S LITERARY CRITICISM

While in graduate school at Cambridge in the 1970s, Gates began to analyze the writings of African and African-American authors published in English between the eighteenth and twentieth centuries. Under the direction of Professor John Holloway, Gates began to experiment with the application of contemporary theories of literary criticism to black literature. This early work at Cambridge formed the foundation upon which much of his future work of literary analysis would be built.

Gates began his study by examining the content of black literature written during the Harlem Renaissance. This period in American artistic history, also known as the New Negro Renaissance, is characterized by a proliferation of achievements in the arts by African Americans. Gates's objective was to ascertain whether African-American literature could be examined, analyzed, and explicated, using the same contemporary styles of literary criticism that were used in English literature.

As the first and only black graduate student at Cambridge at the time, Gates found himself personalizing his interpretations. His analysis was slanted towards what the text was saying to him, an African-American living in a racist society, as opposed to what the author might have been communicating to society as a whole. He also saw a difference in the way he viewed black literature versus works written by white authors. The latter soon came to be "intellectual play" for him, while analyzing black texts proved to be both personal and political. According to Gates:

> . . . literary theory functioned in my education as a prism, which I could turn to refract different spectral patterns of language use in a text, as one does with daylight. Turn the prism this way, and one pattern of color emerges; turn it that way, and another pattern configures. Early on, it was the play of the spectra of language in a text that motivated me to study the history of criticism. In this way, I learned fairly systematically about the history and theory of criticism. . . .

Gates found racism inherent in the contemporary critical theories being used to study literature. Often referred to as "Western traditions," these theories reflected literary analysis from the perspective of being white, male, and Western (European). Gates's work with black literature led to the development of black text-specific theories which rely on black tradition to critically analyze a text in the cultural context in which it is written, then translate contemporary theories to the work to produce more meaningful bodies of literature.

Gates's fascination with black literary theory has centered on language. In the book *Figures in Black: Words, Signs and the Racial Self* he writes: "For it is language, the black language of black texts, that expresses the distinctive quality of our literary tradition."

Gates writes: "Much of my work in black criticism arises from my analysis of the racist uses to which the absence of black writing has been put since the eighteenth century. . . . [I] realized that the black tradition's own concern with winning the war against racism had led it not only to accept this arbitrary relationship but to embrace it, judging its own literature by a curious standard that derived from social applications of the metaphors."

Gates wanted to step outside the realm of familiarity that occurred when a black critic read a black text, an experience he himself underwent. He wanted to study black literature for the experience and not as a mirror image of his own life.

AFRICAN-AMERICAN LITERATURE

Until the later part of the twentieth century, African-American literature had been considered unimportant and irrelevant. Traditionally, the black writer has been limited in scope of experiences, which in turn, has limited the availability and depth of subject matter. Until recent times, prospective black authors have had limited numbers of established African-American authors to whom they could look for creative perspective and direction. As a result, they turned to the works of white writers for guidance in format as well as subject matter.

The writings of many notable early African-American writers, such as John Smith and Jonathan Edwards, are not usually found in the literature books studied by students. According to one African-American literary scholar Lindsay Patterson, ". . . the black writer has been cheated out of a wellspring; but more than that, he has been made to feel that his ancestors contributed only a 'shuffling' stereotype to the literary developments in this country."

The first African-American authors, seventeenth century slaves, were for the most part religious writers of sermons; they did not write much about slavery or other social conditions. As slavery became more widespread and accepted, many of the African Americans who were able to write, wrote of their experiences as slaves or escaping slavery. These works were often graphic in their representation of the brutality of slavery, and abolitionists used them to aid their struggle to end slavery. According to Patterson, uncovering the hundreds of pre-Civil War tracts, letters, sermons, and narratives would reveal the life of the African Americans unlike that portrayed in the history books. Slaves wrote to let their voices be heard and to legitimatize their existence. It is believed that early African-American slave writers shared their work with one another and read one another's writings.

Many blacks writing around the time of the Civil War had little or no formal education. Others, such as Phillis Wheatley, were educated by their owners and wrote and sometimes published their own material. One type of black literary tradition, the narrative, was used by slaves to interpret the human experience. (A literary tradition is a way of writing.) Narratives relate significant events, whether fiction or nonfiction. The narratives and stories of Africans brought in bondage to the New World are thought to represent the beginning of the Afro-America Literary tradition. Literature has always been associated with culture. The early slave narratives, however, were written less to enhance culture and more to prove literary ability. One of the literary theories Gates has tried to espouse is that black culture constitutes an essential element of American culture.

According to Gates: ". . . After [philosopher, René] Descartes, reason was privileged over all other human characteristics, and writing was taken to be the visible sign of reason. Blacks were reasonable, and hence 'men,' only if they could demonstrate mastery of the 'arts and sciences'—that is, writing," Gates continued:

> Literacy stood as the ultimate measure of humanity for those struggling to define an African self in Western letters; their project was to establish a collective black voice through the sublime example of an individual text, and thereby to register a black presence in letters.

Believed to be inferior to whites, slaves were forbidden to learn to read and write—they did so under a penalty of death. The urge to create a literary work was an expression of a need to connect with humanity. Black narrative writing was at the height of its productivity and popularity between 1850-1859.

Phillis Wheatley's *Poems on Various Subjects, Religious and Moral* became the first book of poetry published by an African American in the English language. This marked the beginning of an African-American literary tradition. Wheatley, born in 1753, was taken from Africa and sold into slavery when she was seven years old. She was purchased by kind people in Massachusetts, who taught her how to read and write. After it was published, *Poems on Various Subjects, Religious and Moral* was widely reviewed and discussed in both Europe and America, and Wheatley became the most popular African-American of her times. In 1774, the Wheatley's gave Phillis her freedom. Thomas Paine published one of her poems in his *Pennsylvania Magazine* in April 1776.

Early scholars of black literature attempted to use their studies to disprove and contest racism, and the anti-slavery coalition offered Wheatley's poetry as proof of the equality of African abilities. In 1849, William G. Allen, the publisher of Phillis Wheatley's poems, said: "The African's called inferior. But what race has ever displayed intellect more exaltedly, or character so sublime?"

The first novel written by an African American was *Clotel: Or the President's Daughter*, by William Wells Brown. It was first published in England in 1853 and then published in an edited form in the United States in 1867. Around this same time, blacks oppressed by slavery began to use poetry as a means of expressing their angst.

The early twentieth century brought black writers into their own. The Harlem Renaissance in the 1920s became known as "Harlem's Golden Age." Instead of imitating white writers, black writers began experimenting with their own writing techniques, resulting in the formation of their own collective voice. Their work, freed from previous themes of slavery, emerged as commentary of evolving African-American life, centering on topics with greater human appeal and issues that pertained to all humankind. A distinction in writing was made. The African-American writer was ". . . encouraged by reviewers, [and] assured that his talent was genuine, that he was just not a Negro writer, but a writer who happened to be Negro, that his first book had broken new ground, and that his next would be awaited with keen interest."

Unlike black musicians, who found ready acceptance in their work, black writers, particularly writers of fiction, did not. Bookstores resisted stocking works by blacks, and readers were opposed to literature that contained racial overtones. Audiences scrutinized the black author's points of view and searched for traditional racial attitudes, but for different reasons. White readers saw societal acceptance when traditional roles were used in writing, while the black reader saw them as the continuation and condoning of societal roles of which he was a part. Arna Bontemps said: "The Negro writer, like the white writer of the South, is a product of the Southern condition. Whether he wills it or not, he reflects the tensions and cross-purposes of that environment. Just as the myth of the Old South weakens under close examination, the myth of literature divorced from what have been called sociological considerations dissolves in a bright light."

GATES'S SIGNIFYING THEORY

Gates caused controversy over his interpretation of black literary theory when he proposed a separate standard for black literature. He was challenged by critics who questioned the motive behind wanting to establish such a standard.

One of the ways Gates strives to define traditions of African-American writing is by detaching it from European influence. Gates's attempt to canonize black literature has been called "racist, separatist, nationalist, or essentialist." One of the reasons Gates feels black literature has historically been excluded from other bodies of literature is that white art takes its origin from Western or European culture, and that black literature cannot be judged on the same basis as white literature—from a European point of view. Gates does not confine his opinion of the need for inclusion solely to literature. "There must be systems that account for the full complexity of American art, music and literature in all their multicultural strains . . . to say that black art is a thing apart, separate from the whole is a racist fiction. We have to conceive a new aesthetic status for American art in all of its facets."

In 1989, Gates defined his approach to critiquing African-American literature utilizing separate cultural criteria in his book, *The Signifyin(g) Monkey: Towards a Theory of Afro-American Literary Criticism*, for which he won a 1989 American Book Award. He based his theories of signifying on the work of other literary scholars who had previously studied signifying as a component of linguistic literature, or connected with the Afro-American literary tradition.

One of the theories of black literary criticism that Gates espouses in *The Signifyin(g) Monkey* has to do with the black vernacular, or manner of speaking. Gates's choice in names for his theory—"signifying" illuminates the very principle to which he wishes to call attention. When writing *The Signifyin(g) Monkey*, Gates proposed the theory that many cultural elements that present-day African Americans consider part of their culture have actually been handed down through the generations by way of Africa. Using black vernacular as an example, he traced the use of signifying to its African roots.

In the eighteenth and nineteenth centuries, slaves often resisted learning the language of their white masters, and according to Gates, created their own vernacular, or manner of speaking. Enclosing the "g" in parenthesis in the book's title emphasizes the difference in speech between pronouncing the hard "g" or dropping it, as happens in vernacular speech. Gates believes that to truly understand black literature, one must first understand the black vernacular in which words can have double meanings: one meaning according to a black translation, and one according to a white translation. "Signifying is my metaphor for literary history," wrote Gates.

At the core of the signifying theory is his explanation that words spoken or written must be understood in terms of cultural context. Reading involves interpreting words rather than absorbing them and becomes an individualistic act rather than a forced understanding of what is being read, as characterized by the writer. In this context, the word *signify* means "suggestion or implication." In Western traditions of literary analysis, the word *signify* means to specifically define a word or idea. Gates sees the Western application of signifying as contrary to the very freedoms implied in the act of writing.

John Wideman, reviewing *The Signifyin(g) Monkey* in a *New York Times* book review, called signifying ". . . verbal play that serves as instruction, entertainment, mental exercise, preparation for interacting with friend and foe in the social arena. In black vernacular, signifying is a sign that words cannot be trusted, that even the most literal utterance allows room for interpretation, that language is both carnival and a minefield."

DEFENDING HIP HOP

In 1990, Gates used his theory of signifying when he helped defend the hip-hop group, 2 Live Crew, against obscenity charges in their First Amendment trial. The Miami, Florida, group was accused of singing songs containing obscenities on their album, *As Nasty As They Wanna Be,* and a Broward County Florida judge's ruling made it the first record in the United States to be declared legally obscene. Gates defended 2 Live Crew's right to free speech by applying his theory of signifying to the band's music. In Gates's opinion, 2 Live Crew's lyrics consisted of "great humor, great joy, and great boisterousness. It's a joke. It's a parody and parody is one of the most venerated forms of art." Citing his theory of signifying, Gates warned against taking the lyrics of the song literally.

". . . The very large question of obscenity and the First Amendment cannot even be addressed until those who would answer them become literate in the vernacular traditions of African Americans," Gates wrote in an article for the *New York Times*.

Because of his defense of 2 Live Crew, some of Gates's critics feel he wishes to endorse the black cultural voice to the exclusion of Western culture or take African-American works out of the context of the culture that produced them. Very much aware that black culture constitutes an essential element of American culture, Gates works to interconnect both spheres. He is a champion of tolerance, and he stresses the importance of values and traditions of all cultures and argues for the need to create a civic culture that honors people's similarities and differences. "The challenge facing America will be the shaping of a truly common public culture, one responsive to the long-silenced cultures of color," Gates explains. He envisions values and traditions intertwined with culture, and he insists that standards be followed when studying these issues, always looking for the link between African-American influences in the multicultural environment. Gates believes that multicultural differences in society need to be honored, and he cites the multicultural setting of his own early roots as forming the basis for his beliefs.

According to Gates, in order to tolerate a culture you have to understand it. He would like to see the public educational system apply scholarly standards and principles to these issues. Gates feels the American education system must be revised to include works produced by non-Western cultures, and he is critical of those who deny America's

Much of Gates's academic writing about literature takes a wide ranging, multicultural view, embracing both the Western literary traditions
as well as African-American traditions. He believes that the American
educational system must begin to embrace work by non-Western cultures if we are to remain a truly plural nation.

multicultural past and present. "Americans must learn to
live without the age-old deleterious dream of purity,
whether purity of blood lines or purity of cultural inheri-
tance."

Calling the differences in approaches to black literature
the "culture wars," Gates tries to take a central view. In his
writing as well as his critical analysis, Gates supports
Western traditions, while arguing for wide-ranging and
varied multicultural approaches, especially towards

African-American literature. "Society simply won't survive without the values of tolerance, says Gates. "And cultural tolerance comes to nothing without cultural understanding."

"I wouldn't want to get rid of anything in [the Western] tradition. I think the Western tradition has been a marvelous, wonderful tradition. But it's not the only tradition full of great ideas," Gates has said. He further states that there can be no doubt that white texts inform and influence black texts (and vice versa), so that a thoroughly integrated canon of American literature is not only politically sound, it is intellectually sound. According to Gates: "If we relinquish the ideal of America as a plural nation, we've abandoned the very experiment America represents."

6

Following in
Du Bois's Footsteps

"Black intellectuals who wish to set an example must
confront the twin realities of white racism . . . and our
own failures to take the initiative and break the cycle
of poverty. . . ."

—Henry Louis Gates, Jr., Presidential
Lecture and Symposia in the Humanities
and Arts, Stanford University,
October 12, 1998

After four productive years at Yale University, Gates was
refused tenure. Disappointed, he left Yale and, in the
beginning of the fall term of 1985, became a full professor
of English and African Studies at Cornell University.
Around the same time, Kwame Anthony Appiah also left
Yale and joined Gates at Cornell. In 1988, Gates made history when he was appointed the W.E.B. Du Bois Professor

68

Like his inspirational mentor W.E.B. Du Bois (seen here in this picture), who was the first African American to receive a Ph.D. from Harvard University, Gates, too, became a "first" in 1979. In that year, Gates became the first African American to receive a Ph.D. from Cambridge University in England.

of Literature at Cornell. It was the first time an African-American male had held an endowed chair in Cornell University's history.

When Henry Louis Gates, Jr. became the first African American to receive a Ph. D. from Cambridge University in England in 1979, he was following in the footsteps of his mentor, W.E.B. Du Bois, the first African American to earn a doctorate degree in history at Harvard University. Half a century before the work of Dr. Martin Luther King, Jr. was influencing African-American lives, Du Bois was championing civil rights and full inclusion of black citizens into American society.

W.E.B. DU BOIS

William Edward Burghardt Du Bois was born in 1863 in Great Barrington, Massachusetts, and raised by a single mother until her death when he was 17 years old. While in high school, Du Bois worked as a correspondent for the *New York Globe*. Even at this young age, Du Bois felt the need to use writing to encourage members of his race to improve their living conditions.

In 1884, Du Bois became the first African American to receive a diploma at his high school. He aspired to attend Harvard University, but when his mother died, he was sent on a Congregational Church scholarship to Fisk University, a prestigious college for blacks in Nashville, Tennessee. There, Du Bois encountered the poverty, violence, and racial prejudice of the South. Du Bois's years at Fisk gave him the opportunity to experience a socio-political climate much different than the one he had known in Massachusetts. These impressions were to remain with him for the rest of life and often found their way into his socio-political and culturally-conscious writings.

Du Bois eventually transferred to Harvard and received a second bachelor's degree before going on to graduate studies in history. In 1892, with funds he received from a fellowship, Du Bois transferred to Fredrich Wilhelm University in Berlin, Germany. He was intent on obtaining a doctoral degree in sociology and economics. When his funding expired, Du Bois was forced to return to Harvard. While he was reluctant to come back to the United States, he also saw the cessation of his funds as a sign that he was meant to be in America. He wrote in his journal that it was time for him "to make a name in science, to make a name in literature, and, thus, to raise my race." He undertook a life-long goal to study racial prejudice. To Du Bois, prejudice was the "problem of the twentieth century."

In 1894, Du Bois became the first African American to receive a doctorate in history from Harvard. He divided his time between writing and lecturing, and quickly established himself as a black intellectual.

The first opportunity for Du Bois to study the black social system in America came in 1896, when, with a grant from the University of Pennsylvania, he researched the slums of Philadelphia. Using a scientific approach, Du Bois combined the disciplines of anthropology, history, sociology, and statistics to complete his study. This was the first time a scientific approach had been employed this way, and because of it, Du Bois became known as "Father of Social Science."

Du Bois' most influential book, *Souls of Black Folk*, was published in 1903, when he was 35 years old. After its publication, Du Bois was considered the second greatest African-American intellectual, following in the footsteps of Frederick Douglass.

In 2000, Gates wrote about his mentor in his book, *The African American Century: How Black Americans Have Shaped Our Country*, which he co-authored with Cornel West. In this book, Gates sums up the sociological impact of *Souls of Black Folk*:

> Part sociology, part history, part polemic, and part creative literature, *Souls* proposed to give voice to the 'nation-within-a-nation' that was the eight mil-

lion Americans of African-American descent. Through myth and metaphor, and in a lyrical yet polemical prose, the young Du Bois charted the contours of the civilization—the arts and sciences, the metaphysical and religious systems, the myths and music, the social and political institutions, the history both before and after Emancipation—that defined a truly African-American culture at the outset of the new century.

In 1909, Du Bois founded the National Association for the Advancement of Colored People (NAACP) and served as the organization's director of publications and research for 24 years. As such, he served as editor-in-chief for the agency's magazine, *Crisis*, which featured the work of early twentieth century academics and artists.

In 1919, Du Bois traveled to France to organize a Pan-African conference to address the issues Africans were facing worldwide. For the next 40 years, Du Bois remained at the forefront of the African-American intellectual community. He joined the Communist Party and was ordered by the United States Department of Justice to register as a "foreign principal" for demanding that atomic weapons be outlawed. He traveled widely and wrote prolifically on the dangers of racism, imperialism, and oppression of all kinds.

Du Bois spent the final year of his life living in Ghana as a citizen. When he died in 1964, at the age of 91, he was working on *Encyclopedia Africana*, a compilation of African culture and history. He died the evening before the historic march on Washington, D.C., when 250,000 people came out to show support for the Civil Rights Bill proposed by President John F. Kennedy and to hear Dr. Martin Luther King, Jr. deliver his famous "I Have a

Dream" speech. About Du Bois, Dr. Martin Luther King, Jr. wrote:

> History cannot ignore W.E.B. Du Bois because history has to reflect truth and Dr. Du Bois was a tireless explorer and a gifted discoverer of social truths. His singular greatness lay in his quest for truth about his own people. There were very few scholars who concerned themselves with honest study of the black man and he sought to fill this immense void. The degree to which he succeeded disclosed the great dimensions of the man.

THE TALENTED TENTH

One of the theories Du Bois espoused was called the "Talented Tenth." According to Du Bois, each racial group, would be saved and perpetuated by a small number of exceptional members—just 10 percent. Du Bois said it was the leadership, worthiness, education, and development of the "Talented Tenth" that would benefit the rest of the African race. Du Bois wrote:

> Education and work are the levers to uplift a people. Work alone won't do it unless inspired by the right ideals and guided by intelligence. Education must not simply teach work, it must teach life. The Talented Tenth of the Negro race must be made leaders of thought and mission culture among their people. No others can do this work and Negro colleges must train men for it. The Negro race, like all other races, is going to be saved by its exceptional men.

Gates supports Du Bois's "Talented Tenth" theory of

developing a generation of leaders. A speaker in the 1998 Presidential Lectures and Symposia in the Humanities and Arts, Gates referred to African Americans as "a nation within a nation." He addressed the "Talented Tenth" in his audience, telling them, "we can't pretend any longer that 35 million people will ever possibly be exactly members of the same economic class," and he urged them to "stop feeling guilty about our own success" and make a commitment to serve to those left behind.

"Black intellectuals who wish to set an example must confront the twin realities of white racism on the one hand, and our own failures to take the initiative and break the cycle of poverty on the other," said Gates. Calling leaders who fail to motivate African Americans in innovative and entrepreneurial ways "ethnic cheerleaders," Gates warns that being a leader often involves estrangement and alienation from the very community the leader is trying to help.

Today's "Talented Tenth," Gates told the audience, must strive for reform in employment for adults as well as high school and college students. The risks are needed in the short run, according to Gates, "in order to break a cycle of poverty, despair and hopelessness in the long run."

Gates left Cornell University in 1990 to become the John Spenser Bassett Professor of English at Duke University in Durham, North Carolina. After one year, Gates accepted the invitation to head Harvard University's Department of African-American Studies, which was in its infancy. In 1991, Gates became the W.E.B. Du Bois Professor of the Humanities and the Director of the W.E.B. Du Bois Institute for Afro-American Studies. His Harvard appointments gave him the means of implementing and expanding the vision of his inspirational mentor, W.E.B. Du Bois.

7

Preserving Tradition

> "No one will ever again be able to use the unavailability of black texts as an excuse not to teach our literature."
>
> —Henry Louis Gates, Jr., *Loose Canons*

Very early in his life, Henry Louis Gates, Jr. recognized the importance of his African-American heritage. His brother, Paul Gates, recalls that Gates had an awareness of family and family history even as a child. As an academic scholar, Gates sees himself as a preservationist of African-American literary tradition. His goal is to extend the tradition to all Americans by the verification and documentation of the contributions of African-American writers.

In 1983, while researching and authenticating African-American manuscripts for inclusion in the Black Periodical Literature Project, Gates discovered Harriet E. Wilson's 1859 novel, *Our Nig*. At the time of its discovery, it was believed

Gates has made a life-long commitment to researching and authenticating African American manuscripts. In 1983 Gates began the Black Periodical Literature Project to document and record manuscripts published by early African Americans. The project has come to include more than 40,000 nineteenth century texts.

to be the first novel published by a black woman in the United States. Nearly 20 years later, that honor was given to Hannah Crafts's *The Bondwoman's Narrative*, also rediscovered by Gates.

Originally thought to be written by a white man, *Our Nig* is the story of a free mulatto girl who becomes an indentured servant to a white family in nineteenth century Massachusetts. The story is believed to be the autobiography of Harriet E. Wilson, who wrote the book as a means of earning money to support herself and her son after being abandoned by her husband. The preface begs the reader to purchase the book, stating "Deserted by kindred, disabled by failing health, I am forced to some experiment which shall aid me in maintaining myself and child without extinguishing this feeble life." Six months later, Wilson's son, George Mason Wilson, whom she had placed in a foster home because she was unable to care for him, succumbed to illness and died.

Our Nig was ignored by literary scholars for over 100 years. After Gates rediscovered the work, he painstakingly researched Wilson's life in an attempt to authenticate the author, but precious little about Wilson could be ascertained. Through census records and other documentation, however, Gates was able to conclude that there was indeed a Harriet E. Adams who married a Thomas Wilson, and that events mentioned in the book probably occurred around the time of Wilson's writing.

As Gates continued with the Black Periodical Literature Project, he collected more than 40,000 forgotten nineteenth century texts. Many of these were slave narratives, a genre created by former slaves and used for the most part to promote abolition. Slave narratives are a form of African-American autobiography that document the "peculiar institution" from the inside. Of the estimated 60,000 slaves that successfully escaped bondage, over 100 wrote book-length slave narratives, according to Gates. He has learned that approximately 100 slave narratives were printed as books or pamphlets between 1760 and 1865. Another 100 were published between 1865 and 1930. "Each slave author, in writing about his or her personal life experiences, simultaneously wrote on behalf of the millions of silent slaves still held captive throughout the South," explains Gates.

THE IMPORTANCE OF SLAVE NARRATIVES

African-American literary tradition was born with the slave narrative, which, because of promotion by anti-slavery societies, was widely read both in the United States and overseas in Europe. Many authors of slave narratives promoted their own writings by speaking at abolitionist rallies. Even so, slave authors were not as popular as white writers. As a point of comparison, Gates notes that Harriet Beecher Stowe's anti-slavery novels sold hundreds of thousands more copies than all the black-written slave narratives combined.

The value of slave narratives was first elaborated on in 1846, when Theodore Parker, a theologian, gave a speech he called "The American Scholar." In it, he said:

> Yet, there is one portion of our permanent literature . . . which is wholly indigenous and original . . . that could be written by none but Americans, and only here; I mean the Lives of Fugitive Slaves. But as these are not the work of the men of superior culture they hardly help to pay the scholar's debt. Yet all the original romance of Americans is in them, not in the white man's novel.

In 1852, Charles Sumner, a prominent abolitionist, called the fugitive slaves and their narratives "among the heroes of our age. Romance had no storms of more thrilling interest than theirs. Classical antiquity has preserved no examples of adventurous trial more worthy of renown."

As Gates researched slave narratives, he found that the narrators often took pains to be as precise as possible, and described their experiences in great detail, for fear of being discredited. In addition to slave narratives, a large body of autobiographies, sermons, novels, poetry, and political tracts have survived from the Civil War period.

As in *The Bondwoman's Narrative,* many slave narratives did not specifically describe their routes to freedom. "I cannot describe my journey," Hannah Crafts writes, "my course was due North." Slaves were fearful that after the passage of the Fugitive Slave Law in 1858, slave catchers would come across the Mason-Dixon Line and retrieve runaway slaves. Publishing the details of an escape route could endanger future runaways.

Gates's discovery of *Our Nig* and *The Bondwoman's Narrative* added to the growing interest in black woman's literary tradition. Over the years, African-American women writers have had to fight both racism and sexism. They had long been ignored by black male authors, who claimed that African-American men's writings spoke for all blacks. It has only been in the last quarter of the twentieth century, that black women writers have challenged this presumption on the part of black male authors and forged ahead to create their own literary heritage. As a result, the literary traditions created by black female authors are only now being discovered. According to Gates, the black women's literary movement "already has taken its place as a distinct period in Afro-American literary history, and may even prove to be one of the most productive, as well as sustained."

In 1988, while at Cornell University, Gates published the *Schomburg Library of Nineteenth Century Black Women Writers* for the Schomburg Center for Research in Black Culture in New York City. This work, named for the historian and collection curator Arturo (Arthur) Alfonso Schomburg, has now swelled to over 50 volumes. In publishing this body of work, Gates has preserved the writings of numerous African-American female authors. His work on the Schomburg volume has changed "American cultural thought, demonstrating that black men and black women have never hesitated to grasp the pen and write their own powerful story of freedom."

AFRICAN-AMERICAN LITERARY CANON

In 1990, Gates co-edited the *Norton Anthology of African American Literature* with Nellie Y. McKay, an Afro-American literature professor from the University of Wisconsin. The undertaking, which was 10 years in the making, contains over 2,000 pages and covers a 200-year period. Gates and McKay brought together "essential" texts and "crucially central" authors—those whom they felt to be indispensable to an understanding of the shaping of the tradition, thereby enabling the anthology to more fully represent the various definitions of African-American literary tradition. According to Gates:

> There have been perhaps as many as 160 anthologies of African-American literature published since 1845, but none has been comprehensive enough or large enough to contain the sweep, the range or the depth to encompass a full canon of 250 years of writings in English. . . . What this anthology represents is a first attempt to draw a line between Phillis Wheatley and Toni Morrison. No matter how meandering that line may seem, our hope is to explain how the two are connected formally, internally, and by language, not by ideology, gender or region, and to show how all the texts in between speak to each other.

Gates is aware of the challenge of recovering, recording, and institutionalizing a century's worth of African-American literature. He sees this as a challenge to the student of

As chair of the Afro-American Studies Department at Harvard University, Gates has established a world-class program for the students and scholars alike. Here we see Gates (pictured here on left) on the steps of the Widener Library at Harvard, with fellow scholars Professor K. Anthony Appiah (center) and Professor Harry M. Lasker III.

African-American Studies. "A well-marked anthology functions . . . to create a tradition, and many editors of black anthologies have attempted to include as many black authors and excerpts of their works as possible, in order to preserve and resurrect the tradition, allowing for the works of many authors to survive."

In 1999, Gates and Kwame Anthony Appiah brought the study of African Americans to new levels when they co-edited the 2,000 page volume of *Africana: The Encyclopedia of the African and African American Experience.* With financial support from Microsoft, the two authors also produced an interactive, multimedia CD-ROM encyclopedia of African culture called *Encarta Africana,* fulfilling Du Bois's dream of creating a single resource where students of African subjects could learn about the people, culture, and history of blacks throughout the world. Its release has elevated the importance of African-American Studies in the United States.

Gates is the author and editor of numerous other books and articles. It is his hope that the literary canons and traditions he is working to recover and create will define African-American literature for students, as well as educators who wish to teach African-American literature. Says Gates, "No one will ever again be able to use the unavailability of black texts as an excuse not to teach our literature."

8

The Wonders
of Africa

> "My quest to encounter the glories of Africa's past
> would be a journey of discovery; for the readers and
> viewers... [and] for me as well."
>
> —Henry Louis Gates, Jr.,
> *Wonders of the African World*

Gates's fascination with Africa, which began in the fifth grade, has stayed with him throughout his life. As a child, Gates absorbed all he could about the continent. He read about *New York Times* journalist Henry Morton Stanley's rescue of British explorer David Livingstone in 1871. The story of Cecil Rhodes, the prime minister of Cape Colony in South Africa, after whom the country of Rhodesia is named, captivated him, as did the discoveries of archeologists, Mary and L.S.B Leakey, whose East African digs brought significant archeological findings to light. Yet, all of the information about Africa that Gates gleaned from his books and the evening news wasn't enough. He longed to see Africa with his own eyes. This wish was first fulfilled in 1970, when, as a student, Gates traveled to Tanzania to work in the mission hospital.

Gates's expectations about his trip were formed by reading W.E.B. Du Bois's 1923 account of his first visit to the continent of Africa, which Gates read in his sophomore year at college. Du Bois had written:

> When shall I forget the night I set foot on African soil? I am the six generation in descent from forefathers who left this land. . . . The spell of Africa is upon me. The ancient witchery of her medicine is burning my drowsy, dreamy blood. This is not a country, it is a world, a universe of itself and for itself, a thing Different, Immense, Menacing, Alluring. It is a great black bosom where the spirit longs to die.

GATES IN AFRICA

After his initial journey in 1970, Gates returned to Africa several times. In 1994, Gates and his family embarked upon a 3,000-mile rail trip through Zimbabwe, Zambia, and Tanzania to film an episode for *Great Railway Journeys* for the British Broadcasting Company and Public Broadcasting System. While traveling the continent, he conceived of an idea for a film series and companion book about ancient African civilizations and their lost wonders. Gates envisioned the series being an African version of "The Seven Wonders of the World." He solicited suggestions from those who study African culture worldwide and came up with a list of places in Africa that fit into the category of "wonder." Gates felt he could visit all of the wonders suggested in six visits to Africa. "My quest to encounter the glories of Africa's past would be a journey of discovery; for the readers and viewers,...[and] for me as well."

HENRY LOUIS GATES, JR.
THE WONDERS OF AFRICA

Gates began filming the series in 1998. To traverse the African terrain, he and his crew traveled by Land Cruiser, truck, canoe, camel, and dhow (an Arab sailing vessel). In an attempt to learn about the African people and their contributions to civilization, Gates interviewed an array of Africans, from kings to archaeologists, from local taxi drivers to imams. He was especially interested in learning what the African people had been like before European explorers enslaved and kidnapped them and colonized their land.

"I knew that any meaningful explanation of what Africa was to me would depend on discovering what Africa was, and is, both to Africans and to all of us, to the world's great family of questioning peoples," he said.

According to Gates, the majority of Americans do not equate Africa with great ancient civilizations. Over the years, the term "African" has come to denote a race as well as a geographical location. Gates strove to dispel the mindset that views Africa as a land overwhelmed by poverty, disease, famine, and war. He wanted to rediscover Africa's majesty and its ancient civilizations, and to strip away preconceived attitudes and labels imposed on the continent by Europe and the Western world. He wanted to show Africa as it truly is and was, and not as it is thought to be.

Gates wrote, "Modern Africa consists of fifty-one countries. Its people speak some 1,500 languages . . . yet we often speak about 'Africa' as if it were a single country in which people speak one indigenous language."

Gates traveled across the Sudan's Nubian Desert from the capital city of Khartoum to Delgo. Following in the footsteps of European explorers and ancient trade routes, he searched the Ethiopian Highlands for the lost Ark of the Covenant. He visited civilizations which were once the most sophisticated of any known to man. These included Nubia's ancient empire, which around 780 B.C. ruled Egypt, and where the oldest urban site known in Africa—Kerma—is located.

Working with photographer Lynn Davis, Gates felt challenged to find a way to "let the African past speak in its own terms, in its own multiplicity of voices, to an audience of Westerners, both black and white. The result is a six hour Public Broadcasting System documentary, Wonders of the African World with Henry Louis Gates, Jr., and a companion book.

Through both the video and the book, Gates shows a side of Africa rarely studied by Westerners by revealing two aspects of the continent. the categories old civilizations whose historical significance has for the most part been forgotten, as well as modern-day Africans eager to embrace the twenty-first century. He has opened the eyes of the world to the African legacy that belongs to all the civilizations of the world and has elevated it to that of the civilizations of ancient Greece and Rome. In doing so, Gates has shown that not only is Africa the birthplace of the ancestors of African Americans; it is a place that has enriched and enhanced world civilization.

9

Realizing
the Vision

> "But the thing I'm proudest of is that for us Afro-Americans, it is not only making a contribution to African American Studies. . . . We are transforming the traditional disciplines as well. The notion of what constitutes the canon of American literature is fundamentally different now because of the growth of Afro-American Studies . . ."
>
> —Henry Louis Gates, Jr., Interview
> with Bruce Cole of the National Endowment
> of the Humanities, after being selected the 2002
> Jefferson Lecturer in the Humanities.

Harvard University opened the Department of Afro-American Studies in the 1970s. As head of the department, Henry Louis Gates, Jr. is one of the most respected and esteemed scholars in the United States. Under his direction, the department has grown from a one-professor course of study to a vibrant and nationally respected branch of the university. Currently over 1,000 students are enrolled in African-American Studies at Harvard, and they are taught by more than 50 professors. In the fall semester of 2002, Harvard University achieved a historic milestone when it admitted its first class of students preparing for graduate degrees in African-American Studies.

The field of African-American Studies has benefited from Gates's dedication. Because of his research into long-lost writings, and his literary scholarship and criticism, the academic discipline has come to be widely recognized and respected. Gates has put new emphasis on African-American culture by his teaching, archival studies, and literary scholarship. His writings and research have given African American Studies throughout the United States credibility and have allowed a new area of study, once considered merely "politically correct," to flourish into a viable academic discipline.

BUILDING A GREAT DEPARTMENT

At Harvard University, Gates has tried to create the greatest center of African-American Studies in the country. When he was first appointed in 1991, Gates saw his first challenge as building a great department. "When I [first] came to Harvard, there was only one professor and one student [in the department of Afro-American Studies.]. I've hired all [the professors in the department], except the one person who was here."

Upon accepting his position at Harvard, Gates told University President Neil L. Rudenstine that for Harvard to become a major center for African-American Studies, an archive comparable to that at Yale, which was considered the standard at the time, was needed. Gates went out and established an archive that was visual, documentary, and literary by purchasing significant documents and photographs. The archive at Harvard now holds the papers of Wole Soyinka, Albert Murray, Chinua Achebe, and John Wideman, and the papers belonging to Du Bois's second wife, Shirley Graham Du Bois.

Gates's first priority as department head, however, was to build an Afro-American Studies Department. ". . . I couldn't really do the kind of archival research that I wanted to do, particularly in the first four or five years that I was here because it was such hard work building the department," Gates remembers. He understands that any qualified scholar—not just an African American—is capable of teaching African-American Studies and black literature. The faculty he has selected to teach in his department is diverse in culture and ethnicity. They have varied academic backgrounds, ranging from law to anthology to music. Each member is involved in an assortment of research interests integral to the African-American experience.

About himself, Gates says: "I am a literary critic. That's the first descriptor that comes to mind. After that I would say I was a teacher. Both would be just as important." Gates also calls himself a lover of archives and sees himself as someone who is dedicated to resurrecting texts that have been forgotten or lost. He likens his role as an African-American scholar to a Talmudic scholar in the Jewish tradition, whose job is to preserve and resurrect texts, and then explain them to the community. He finds challenges in balancing his love of archival studies, teaching, and being a department administrator.

"Skip brings unsurpassed commitment, energy, and creativity to [the African-American experience]," said Lawrence H. Summers, current president of Harvard

University. "His extraordinary scholarship, vision, and commitment have helped to make Harvard's Afro-American Studies department pre-eminent in the nation. His charisma, leadership, and unbounded energy have touched the lives of faculty and students across . . . the entire University."

Homi K. Bhabha, Ph.D., the Anne F. Rothenberg Professor of English and American literature and a Professor of African-American Studies at Harvard, has been a colleague and a collaborator with Gates for over 20 years. Of Gates he says: " . . . he is a remarkable Chair, a hirer of excellent people who has brought together the most remarkable group of scholars."

Gates currently teaches one graduate and one under-graduate course a year. Three of the courses he consistently teaches are on the Harlem Renaissance, a course on African-American Women's Writing, and a course on African-American literary tradition. His choice of courses finds its foundation in the words of his late mentor, John Blassingame, who taught him to "teach what you write, write what you teach." Gates has further refined Blassingame's advice to prepare research and present it in a lecture format several times prior to publishing, in order to refine it, and discover its flaws, before it goes into print.

Gates's goal at Harvard is to work towards "what I hope will be the greatest center of intellection concerning persons of African descent in the Old World and the New World." One of the agencies that has been particularly helpful in providing the funding African-American research at Harvard is the National Endowment for the Humanities, which has provided the funding to support the research needed for Gates to realize his vision.

As the Director of the W.E.B. Du Bois Institute for

Afro-American Research, Gates is responsible for awarding between 10 and 15 fellowships annually to scholars in the fields of African and African-American Studies. The institute also promotes lectures, reading, conferences, and forums, and sponsors research and publication projects. Recognizing the need to be committed to the community, the institute also subsidizes the Martin Luther King, Jr. After-School Program, in which teachers work with inner-city middle school and high school students to teach them African and African-American history and culture. The W.E.B Du Bois Society, another program sponsored by the W.E.B. Du Bois Institute, allows Harvard professors and students to reach out to students in the community to assist them in developing study skills, including computer skills, and teamwork building.

In July of 2002, two of Gates's long-time colleagues and collaborators, Kwame Anthony Appiah and Cornel West, left Harvard University to continue their academic careers at Princeton University in New Jersey. Gates was invited by his two colleagues to join them at Princeton. Appiah had several times changed his university association to follow Gates, and Gates seriously considered whether it was time to return the favor. In the end, Gates elected to stay at Harvard, stating in a press release that "because of my devotion to the department and the Du Bois Institute, I felt it crucial that I remain here and join . . . in this exciting process of rebuilding."

Gates sometimes comes across to his academic peers as more of a celebrity than an academic because of his visibility and newsworthiness. Indeed, fellow academics sometime criticize him for this. Gates represents a new blend of a member of academia, and his critics often complain that is hard to tell whether Gates is a public intellectual in an academic environment or an academic intellectual in the public limelight.

As a lover of African and African-American art, both as a scholar and collector, Gates views art as an integral part of African-American Studies. As chair of the Afro-American Studies department at Harvard, he has hired art historians as professors. Gates has served on Boards of Trustees for several art galleries, including the Museum of Fine Arts and the Whitney, and has many personal friends who are art historians. He promotes the integration of African-American art into his work.

Gates continues to be outspoken and air his views about American society in general, and African-American society in particular. On the subject of education, he opposes a strict theory of intellectual racism that says blacks are intellectually inferior. However he opposes curricula that focus on any one single culture. Gates feels that schools should teach only African American culture and endorse racism, and he would like to see an American educational system that includes the contributions produced by all non-Western cultures.

> I rebel at the notion that I can't be part of other groups, that I can't construe identities through objective affinity, that race must be the most important thing about me. Is that what I want on my gravestone. Here lies an African American? So I'm divided. I want to be black, to know black, to luxuriate in whatever I might be calling blackness at any particular time— but to do so in order to come out the other side, to experience a humanity that is neither colorless nor reducible to color.

Gates has been the recipient of numerous awards and honors. Here we see Gates with former President Bill Clinton during a presentation of the 1998 National Medal of Arts and the National Humanities Medal Awards. Gates was one of the award recipients that year.

GATES'S LEGACY

Gates has been instrumental in changing the way students view literary history in academia. He has also brought the study of literary history to the forefront through the many critical texts and republished works he has edited, as well as the lost manuscripts he has discovered.

"But the thing I'm proudest of is that for us Afro-Americans, it is not only making a contribution to African-American Studies. . . . We are transforming the traditional disciplines as well. The notion of what constitutes the canon of American literature is fundamentally different now because of the growth of Afro-American Studies . . . "

Gates is also concerned with the representation of blacks on television, which he calls a "very poor index to our social advancement or political progress." He is also concerned about the attitude of blacks towards education and athletics, and he speaks out against the glorification of sports as a substitute for education "as if they were classrooms in an alternative school system."

Gates holds 40 honorary degrees and has received dozens of awards. In 1997, *Time* magazine named him one of the "25 Most Influential Americans," and in 1998, President Bill Clinton presented him with a National Humanities Award.

Going forward into the twenty-first century, Gates will continue to inform and enlighten both his students as well as the American public about issues that are fundamental and vital to the African-American experience. With a lifetime of accomplishments behind him, he will certainly go down in history, like his inspirational mentor W.E.B. Du Bois, as one of the greatest African-American intellectuals of all time.

Chronology

1983   Discovers and reissues *Our Nig*, which was at the time the earliest known novel published by an African-American female.

1984–1985   Appointed Associate Assistant Professor of English and Afro-American Studies, Yale University. *Black Literature and Literary Theory*, Gates's first book, is published.

1985   Appointed Professor of English, Comparative Literature and Africana Studies at Cornell University.

1988   *Schomburg Library of Nineteenth Century Black Women Writers* is published. Named W.E.B. Du Bois Professor of Literature at Cornell University.

1990   Becomes John Spencer Bassett Professor of English and Literature, Duke University. Defends 2 Live Crew in their Florida obscenity trial. Co-edits *Norton Anthology of African American Literature*.

1991   Appointed W.E.B. Du Bois Professor of Humanities and Director of the W.E.B Du Bois Institute for Afro-American Research and Chair of Afro-American Studies Department at Harvard University.

1998   Travels to Africa six times in 12 months to film *Wonders of the African World with Henry Louis Gates, Jr.* and writes the companion book *Wonders of the African World*, to accompany the video.

1999   Co-edits 2,000 page volume of *Africana: The Encyclopedia of the African and African American Experience*, which is later released on CD as *Encarta Africana*.

2001   Discovers *The Bondwoman's Narrative*, believed to be the earliest known novel written by an African-American female slave.

Bibliography

Bigelow, Barbara Carlisle. *Contemporary Black Biography.* Volume 3. Detroit: Gale Research, 1993.

Bontemps, Arna. "The Negro Renaissance: Jean Toomer and the Harlem Writers of the 1920s" *International Library of African American Life and History: An Introduction to Black Literature in America, from 1746 to the Present.* Lindsay Patterson ed. New York: The Association For the Study of Afro-American Life and History, 1978.

Cole, Bruce. "Interview: Henry Louis Gates, JR., 2002 Jefferson Lecturer in the Humanities." *http://www.neh.gov/whoweare/gates/interview*

Crafts, Hannah. *The Bondwoman's Narrative.* New York: Warner Books, Inc., 2002.

Delbanco, Andrew. "Talking Texts," The *New Republic.* January 9, 16, 1989.

Ervin, Hazel Arnett. *African American Literary Criticism 1773–2000* New York: Twayne Publishers, 1999.

Fisher, Dexter and Robert B. Stepto eds., *Afro-American Literature: The Reconstruction of Instruction.* New York: The Modern Language Association of America, 1978.

Gates, Jr., Henry Louis and Cornel West. *The African American Century: How Black Americans Have Shaped Our Country.* New York: Simon and Schuster, 2000.

Gates, Jr., Henry Louis ed., *Black Literature and Literary Theory.* London: Methuen, 1994.

Gates, Jr., Henry Louis. ed., *The Classic Slave Narratives.* New York: Penguin Putnam, Inc., 2002.

Gates, Jr., Henry Louis. *Colored People: A Memoir.* New York: Alfred A. Knopf, 1994.

Gates, Jr., Henry Louis. *Figures in Black: Works, Signs and the "Racial" Self.* New York: Oxford University Press, 1987.

Gates, Jr. Henry Louis. "The Fugitive." The *New Yorker,* February 18, 25, 2002.

Gates, Jr., Henry Louis. *Loose Canons: Notes on the Culture Wars.* New York: Oxford University Press, 1992.

Gates, Jr., Henry Louis and William L. Andrews. *Pioneers of the Black Atlantic: Five Slave Narratives From the Enlightenment 1772–1815* Washington, D.C. : Counter Point Publishing, 1998 .

Bibliography

Gates, Jr., Henry Louis. ed., *Reading Black, Reading Feminist: A Critical Anthology.* New York: Penguin, Books, Inc. 1990.

Gates, Jr. Henry Louis. *The Signifyin(g) Monkey: A Theory of Afro-American Literary Criticism.* New York : Oxford University Press, 1988.

Gates, Jr., Henry Louis. "Whose Culture Is It Anyway?" The *New York Times.* May 4, 1991.

Gates, Jr., Henry Louis. *Thirteen Ways of Looking at a Black Man.* New York: Random House, 1997.

Gates, Jr., Henry L. "2 Live Crew, Decoded." The *New York Times,* June 6, 1990.

Gates, Jr., Henry Louis. *Wonders of the African World.* New York: Alfred A. Knopf, 1999.

Hynes, Gerald C. "Biographical Sketch of W.E.B. Du Bois" *http://www.duboislc.org/html/DuBoisbio*

Jaehn, Tomas. "Henry Louis Gates, Jr." Stanford Presidential Lectures Website *http://prelectur.stanford.edu/lecturers/g*

Kirkpatrick, David D. "On Long-Lost Pages, a Female Slave's Voice." The *New York Times,* November 9, 2001.

Koolish, Lynda. *African American Writers: Portraits and Visions.* Jackson, Mississippi: University Press of Mississippi, 2001.

Lamb, Brian. "Colored People by Henry Louis Gates, Jr.: Interview." *http://www.booknotes.org/Transcript/?ProgramID=1220*

O'Toole, Kathleen. "Rough Magic of the Cultural Mix is Nation's Best Hope." *http://prelectur.stanford.edu/lectures/gates/jsinterv*

Patterson, Lindsay. *International Library of African American Life and History: An Introduction to Black Literature in America, from 1746 to the Present.* New York: The Association For the Study of Afro-American Life and History, 1978.

Smith, Jessie Carney ed., *Notable Black American Men.* Detroit: Gale, 1998.

Rasmussen, R. Kent ed., *The African American Encyclopedia,* Second Ed. Volume 4. Tarrytown, N.Y.: Marshall Cavendish, 2001.

Wilson, Harriet E. *Our Nig; or, sketches from the life of a Free Black* Henry Louis Gates, Jr., ed. New York: Random House, 1983.

Bibliography

Ziegler, Benjamin Munn ed., *Desegregation and the Supreme Court.* Boston: D.C. Heath and Company, 1958.

Related Web Sites

Transcript of the "Talented Tenth" by W.E.B. Du Bois:
http://teachingamericanhistory.org/library/index.asp?document=

Transcript of Dr. Gates's Emory University Commencement Speech:
http://www/emory.edu/EMORY_MAGAZINE/summer95/commence-
ment.html

CNN Newsmaker Profile:
http://www.cnn/resources/newsmakers/us/newsmakers/henry.gates.html

Dr. Gates's Stanford Presidential Lecture Stanford Presidential Lectures
and Symposia in the Humanities and Arts
http://prelectur.stanford.edu/lectures/gates

Harvard University
http://www.harvard.edu/

Harvard Gazette (article about Dr. Gates and Afro-American Studies)
http://www.news.harvard.edu/gazette/2002/12.05/09-gate

Thompson/Gale Henry Louis Gates, Jr. Biography Website:
wysiwyg://52/http://www.galegroup.com/free_resources/bhm/bio/gates_h

Bass, Patrick Henry and Karen Pugh. *In Our Own Image: Treasured African-American Traditions, Journeys, and Icons.* Philadelphia: Running Press, 2001.

Bloom, Harold (ed.) *Black American Prose Writers of the Harlem Renaissance (Writers of English)* Philadelphia: Chelsea House, 1994.

Bloom, Harold ed., *Black American Prose Writers: Before the Harlem Renaissance* (Writers of English: Lives and Works) Philadelphia: Chelsea House, 1994.

Boyd, Herb ed., *Autobiography of a People: Three Generations of African American History Told by Those Who Lived It.* New York: Random House, 2001.

Brinkley, Douglas. *Rosa Parks.* New York: Viking, 2000.

Douglass, Frederick. *My Bondage and My Freedom.* New York: Penguin, 2003.

Farris, Christine King. *My Brother Martin: A Sister Remembers Growing Up With the Rev. Martin Luther King, Jr.* New York: Simon and Schuster, 2003.

McDaniel, Melissa. *W.E.B. Du Bois: Scholar and Civil Rights Activist.* London: Franklin Watts, 1999.

McKissack, Pat, Patricia C. McKissack, Fredrick L. McKissack. Sojourner Truth: Ain't I A Woman? New York: Scholastic,1994.

Robinson, Cederic, J. *Black Movements in America.* New York: Routledge, 1997.

Somerlott, Robert. *The Little Rock School Desegregation Crisis in American History.* Berkeley Heights: Enslow, 2001.

Wyeth, Sharon, Dennis. *Flying Free: Corey's Underground Railroad Diary.* New York: Scholastic, 2002.

Index

Index

Index

Index

Index

Picture Credits

About the Author

Marylou Morano Kjelle is a freelance writer and photojournalist who lives and works in Central New Jersey. Marylou writes for several local newspapers and has a column in the *Westfield Leader/Times of Scotch Plains-Fanwood* called the "Children's Book Nook" in which she reviews children's books and writes about the love of reading. Marylou holds an M.S. in Science from Rutger's University. She is the author of seven non-fiction books for young readers, many of them biographies. This is her third book for Chelsea House Publishers.